Macroeconomic Issues:

Their Relationship to Fiscal Policy Formulation, Forecasting, Prediction, and Computer Simulation Modeling

by

Nicholas Jewczyn

iUniverse, Inc.
New York   Bloomington

iUniverse books may be ordered through booksellers or by contacting:

iUniverse
1663 Liberty Drive
Bloomington, IN 47403
www.iuniverse.com
1-800-Authors (1-800-288-4677)

Because of the dynamic nature of the Internet, any Web addresses or links contained in this book may have changed since publication and may no longer be valid. The views expressed in this work are solely those of the author and do not necessarily reflect the views of the publisher, and the publisher hereby disclaims any responsibility for them.

ISBN: 978-1-4401-5497-3 (sc)
ISBN: 978-1-4401-5498-0 (ebook)

Library of Congress Control Number: 2009931623

Printed in the United States of America

iUniverse rev. date: 07/07/2009

Cover design by Alysa Butterfield

Dedication

This book is dedicated to my mother, Anastasia, who gave up a promising academic career at university, upon the recommendation of her uncle, in order to marry and start a family. In my youth, she always somehow believed that her bouncing, baby boy would eventually "amount to something."

Forward

Jacob to Esau, ***First sell me your birthright*** (Gen. 25:31) Since the beginning the economy has effectively affected us, even, infected us! If there was a time for economic repentance and economic salvation, it is now! Mr Jewczyn's book is not The Bible, but it is bible-like in that it's a must read for proper understanding of the Economic plight.

Dr. Jason Royle

Abstract

Breadth

The Breadth demonstration consists of a 30-page scholarly paper that critically assesses the three macroeconomic schools of theory as the foundations of modern macroeconomics. The demonstration compares and contrasts the synthesis of economic thought of the three primary economic schools of macroeconomics theory: Adam Smith as the primary theorist of the classicist school; John Maynard Keynes as the primary theorist of the Keynesian school; and Milton Friedman as the primary theorist of the monetarist school (Chicago School of Economics). This demonstration further analyzes several minor theorists who expounded upon these schools of thought and how those enhancements contributed to the three basic theorists' work and to the development of macroeconomics theory. The demonstration evaluates the strengths and limitations of the tenets of macroeconomics theory, as espoused by the principal macroeconomics theorists Smith, Keynes, and Friedman, enlarged upon by the minor theorists. The purpose of these evaluations is to establish how the respective theorists' cumulative, theoretical work has contributed to the development of modern macroeconomics and to the development of a platform of values that is applicable to applied macroeconomics as it relates to economic computer modeling and economic forecasting.

Abstract

Depth

The Depth component of this KAM is comprised of two parts. The first part consists of an annotated bibliography of the 15 cited sources (i.e., refereed journal articles written in the past five years) around the topic objectives stated herein above. Each source annotation is composed of some 1-1 ½ pages. The second part of the Depth component consists of a research literature review essay of some 25-30 pages on the topic.

Abstract

Application

The Application demonstration project is comprised of the development of a theoretical, overall structure of how an economic computer model could be used in a specific application to conduct economic forecasting. The Application component consists of a scholarly essay of about 30 pages, concerning the structure of a prospective model for forecasting, and which critically evaluates this theoretical model in light of the theories from the Breadth and research from the Depth. The theoretical construct will save time, effort, and money, with regard to the formulation of higher quality government fiscal policy intended to alleviate human suffering in the aggregate economy.

TABLE OF CONTENTS

Breadth

Theoretical Macroeconomics

Introduction

The Breadth component of this KAM demonstration compares and contrasts the synthesis of economic thought of the three primary economic schools of macroeconomic theory: Adam Smith as the primary theorist of the classicist school; John Maynard Keynes as the primary theorist of the Keynesian school; and Milton Friedman as the primary theorist of the monetarist school (Chicago School of Economics). Several concepts of the platform of the classicist school of macroeconomics discussed are the: Invisible Hand; liberalism and mercantilism; land and rent; capital and profit; price; labor and wages; and social accounts. These concepts are integral to the understanding of the classicist school of economic thought and are the basis for further discussion in other segments of this paper. Several concepts of the platform of the Keynesian school of macroeconomics discussed are the: liquidity preference; futility of wage reductions; stabilization policy; wage rigidity; the multiplier; and effective demand. These concepts are integral to the understanding of the Keynesian school of economic thought and are the basis for further discussion in other segments of this paper. Several concepts of the platform of the monetarist school of macroeconomics discussed are the: income permanence as the precursor to rational expectations; comparisons of Keynesian Economics, classical Economics and Monetarism; and Friedman's views on banking and the supply of money. These concepts are integral to the understanding of the monetarist school of economic thought and are the basis for further discussion in other segments of this paper. Several minor theorists, who expounded upon these schools of thought and how those enhancements contributed to the three basic theorists' work, are also analyzed to communicate their contributions to the development of macroeconomics theory.

Each of the three principal schools of macroeconomic schools of thought are summarized, analyzed, and contrasted throughout this Breadth segment, but are synthesized into a comparison and contrast of thought in the monetarist portion of the Breadth segment. The demonstration evaluates the strengths and limitations of the tenets of macroeconomics theory, as espoused by the principal macroeconomics theorists Smith, Keynes, and Friedman and enlarged upon by the minor theorists, for the purpose of establishing how their cumulative, theoretical work has contributed to the development of macroeconomics and to the development of a platform of values that is useful in applied macroeconomics as it relates to economic computer modeling and economic forecasting.

Adam Smith and the Classical School of Economics

The Invisible Hand

Smith (1776, 2003) noted that an individual acted in the best interests of the public by engaging in personal self-interest. Smith reasoned that an individual only worked for personal security and governed personal efforts so that the end product was only for personal gain. Smith specifically stated that an individual was "led by an invisible hand to promote an end which was no part of his intention" (p. 572). Smith cautioned that he held those who were supposedly interested in trading for the public good in low esteem because it was "an affectation, indeed, not very common among merchants" (p. 572). Smith also reasoned that the gross revenue of a particular society was the same as that society's annual production that was available to be negotiated in markets. Since the invisible hand was guiding individuals who then contributed to the overall market's value, this competition among individuals was the practical realization of the invisible hand, or competition, which was what optimized a market's overall performance. Smith reasoned that this self-optimization eventually resulted in market optimization and that this market optimization was good for society (p. 572).

Samuelson (1948, 1995) observed, however, that the invisible hand did have limits. The invisible hand only worked in a perfect world where everything was indeed perfect: perfect resource allocation, perfect competition, and efficiently produced finished goods that were equally allocable. If this were actually the case, Samuelson concluded that "there would be no need for government intervention in the economy" (p. 280).

Schumpeter (1942, 2008) echoed the sentiments of Smith when he noted that there were market limiters that could have an effect upon the pursuit of perfect competition. However, this had more to do with cases of monopoly, than with traditional market structures that promoted effective competition in the marketplace. The restriction of competition had an effect upon prices that would then change the market dynamic, preventing perfect competition (p. 78).

Liberalism and Mercantilism

Smith (1776, 2003) explained that there were three distinct obligations owed by a government to its citizens, with regard to regulation and a system of payments. The first was to create and maintain a standing army for national defense. It was Smith's view that this could only be accomplished by the government because the cost to an individual, or group of individuals, was prohibitive (p. 897). Second, the government's obligation was to pay for and maintain a judicial system, so that personal and business interests could be protected and maintained. It was only in this manner that trade and the marketplace could be adequately protected, because of the access to redress of grievances (p. 911). Third, the government was responsible for the maintenance and the original construction of the civil works and institutions for use by the public, because of the prohibitive expense to an individual or group of individuals (p. 916).

Mercantile policy had an impact upon the use of trade. Smith (1776, 2003) insisted that "nothing, however, can be more absurd than this whole doctrine of the balance of trade, upon which, not only these restraints, but almost all the other regulations of commerce are founded" (p. 615). Smith realized that the idea that both sides of a trade came out even, was patently false. Further, even though trade could regularly be carried out between two locations and be profitable, it was incorrect to suppose that this trade would be *equally* profitable for both parties (p. 615). Smith enlarged upon this concept with the idea that, "If a foreign country can supply us with a commodity cheaper than we ourselves can make it, better buy it of them with some part of the produce... employed in a way in which we have some advantage" (p. 573). Ricardo (1817, 2004) referred to this as the law of comparative advantage, resulting from internal workings of specialization, and Samuelson (1948, 1995) said that "this simple principle provides the unshakable basis for international trade" (p. 679).

Land and Rent

Smith (1776, 2003) explained that rent, which was rightfully a payment to the landlord, was the remainder from the complete payment of the expenses to make it possible to cultivate produce. He even advanced the notion that "ground expenses" should be free from a church tithe and free of government taxation. Smith reasoned that if the payment of these ground expenses were to be taxed or tithed, then it would ultimately reduce the amounts payable to both the church and the state. Improvements to the land were a "productive expense," which did not relate to the ground expense, and rent in general had to do with land scarcity (p. 846). Smith further stated that, "High or low wages and profit, are the causes of high or low price; high or low rent is the effect of it" (p. 200). Unfortunately, Smith simply was unable to reconcile the relationship between rent and price.

Ricardo (1817, 2004) grasped the significance of this relationship when he stated, "From the loss of rent there will be a loss of value, of estimated money value, but there will be a gain of wealth. The amount of the raw produce and other productions together will be increased" (p. 291). Ricardo had some intuitive grasp of the fact that real economic production was related to the land rents and it either directly, or indirectly, related the notional value of rent to price. This nullified Smith's idea that per acre rent to the landlord should rise as a proportion, or as a function of, superior acreage output (p. 291).

Samuelson (1948, 1995) explained the land and rent connection very efficiently when he noted that, "The price of using a piece of land for a period of time is called its rent" (p. 243). Rent was just a function of time, and had absolutely nothing to do with the output of the land (described by Smith). Samuelson argued that,

"Rent is the payment for the use of factors of production that are fixed in supply" (p. 243). This was extrapolated from land to all fixed factors of production and became an important foundational issue of macroeconomics (p. 243).

Capital and Profit

There was a connection between capital and profit. Smith (1776, 2003) described that "the capital of an individual can be increased only by what he saves...so the capital of a society, which is the same as all the individuals who compose it, can be increased only in the same manner" (p. 431). Obviously, a profit must first have been made in order to keep savings. So, capital was incremented by the savings of the individual and by society at large (p. 431). Smith connected output, rent, capital, and profit with "produce...from the hands of productive labourers [sic], is destined for replacing a capital, and that which is destined for constituting a revenue, either as rent, or as profit" (p. 426). Savings, as capital, could also be loaned at interest (p. 450). Thus, capital could be increased by savings from profit, and savings could eventually become equal to investment (because savings could be useful in and of itself), or it could be loaned to producers at a given rate of interest.

Although competition (pure or otherwise) could be useful, there was a negative side to that competition. Smith (1776, 2003) explained that an increase in capital could eventually cause profits to diminish, because there would soon not be enough places to invest that capital. So, Smith maintained that greater accumulations of capital would eventually cause the rates of profit to decline, and that competition reduced the amount of profit as low as an industry would stand (before the capital fled elsewhere, due to a lack of returns). However, even though interest rates fall as the "quantity of stock increases," the liquidity movement of that capital, due to increased competition for it, could equalize the rates of that profit among different sectors of industry (p. 451). Smith felt that profit earners had no interest in the general welfare of the economy (and thus as businesspeople should not be trusted), but that those who made a living through the rents and wages were interested in the public welfare and were trustworthy (p. 338). Therefore, those who worked for the public trust (politicians) should not be chosen from the profit earner group, because they did not hold with the general interests of the public and were self-serving (p. 339).

Price

Smith (1776, 2003) realized that monopolists skewed the allocation of the factors of production by purposely providing the markets with a lower supply than what the market demanded. This meant that prices would be inordinately higher than what a consumer, or a producer who used commodities for tillage or manufacturing, would have expected to pay (p. 86). Conversely, "the market price of any particular commodity, though it may continue long above, can seldom continue long below, its natural price" (p. 87). Smith intuitively realized that truly competitive markets, enumerated by the *invisible hand* discussion above, would promote the movement of a market price, eventually, toward the natural price (p. 87). Smith further observed that the "natural price" would directly vary with the component parts of that natural price, which were "wages, profit, and rent" (p. 89).

Marshall (1923, 2003) also realized this component part phenomenon, and mentioned that Cantillon (in 1755) had obliquely referred to this and had added that there were usually some charges that were secondary to the movement of specie that also raised the overall price of a commodity (with regard to silver or gold) (pp. 90, 228). Smith (1776, 2003) concluded that the natural price of a commodity was indicative of its composite parts, and that it was really an aggregate composition of wages, profit, and rent. Another way of stating this was that land, labor, and capital were related to natural price. This concept became a standard, theoretical plank in the platform of classical economics. A further set of notions of classical economics was that, with regard to skewed pricing, commodities for production were removed if the natural price exceeded the market price and continued economic growth eventually removed the skewed pricing (Samuelson 1948, 1995; Marshall, 1923, 2003; Ricardo 1817, 2004).

An important consideration of price could be supply and demand of the commodities in question. Smith (1776, 2003) listed the relationships that culminated with two sides of the same concept: if the supply of the commodity in question was greater than the "effectual demand," then the commodity's market price would be lower than the normal price usually obtained; if the supply of the commodity in question was less than the "effectual demand," then the commodity's market price would be higher than the normal price usually obtained. So, the amount of the difference would then depend upon the nature of the demand (pp. 80-81).

Ricardo (1817, 2004) in his accounting of England's dealings with foreign nations in the trade of such commodities, dealt with this concept (pp. 77-78). The relationship, advanced by Smith (1776, 2003) above and further discussed by Ricardo (1817, 2004), was further elaborated upon by Marshall (1923, 2003) as very plainly, supply and demand. Marshall, to buttress his argument, referred back to Ricardo's *two-nation* hypothetical example of trade, in order to drive home the inter-relationship point of the supply and demand linkage. Marshall further discussed the more advanced notion of the elasticity of demand, predicated upon the commodity's supply, which has become another important plank in the classical economic theoretical platform of today. He predicated his assumptions for this concept upon the fact that "supply is one cause of the elasticity of demand" and "Ricardo's two countries for the goods in general of the other would have considerable elasticity *under modern industrial conditions*" (p. 249).

Labor and Wages

Economic growth could, in some ways, be tied to output. Smith (1776, 2003) documented this view early in his writing with the "pin example." Smith realized that one, unskilled workman laboring to produce an item, one unit of output at a time, would not contribute greatly to the economy. However, once a group of laborers worked in concert, and *specialized* by dividing up the labor functions and performed just a single task each, they would then increase productivity because the *combined* labor productivity would dramatically increase. Smith then extrapolated this concept to all employments and all trades, stating that this division of labor would dramatically increase productivity for any trade or employment (pp. 10-12).

According to Smith (1776, 2003), the main condition that would curb this increase in production would necessarily be the size or demand of the market in question, where the products would then be sold (pp. 10-12). Smith also mentioned that any restrictions upon the free movement of labor, also affected the free movement of capital, and he described these to be in the form of restrictive laws and duties, monopolies, and even the guilds or workman associations. The market was adversely affected by any and all of these and would eventually have the tendency to decrease economic productivity (pp. 185-194). From Smith's views above, we could deduce that the increasing specialization of the labor force would consequently require an increased application of capital and the production advantages from that labor specialization would eventually lead to greater scaled returns (Marshall 1923, 2003).

Smith (1776, 2003) realized that there were several

reasons for the increased productivity attributed to diversified, or specialized, labor to improve the lot of the economy in general. The first reason was that this "diversity of their employment," with regard to that labor, would dramatically then make productive additions to the economy and "to the annual produce of the land and labour [sic] of the country" (p. 458).

Smith (1776, 2003) mixed his thoughts with those of Cantillon for the second of the two reasons. In a static economy, the wages moved toward a basic level that would only support the families of workmen. This maintained the population of workers over time, but didn't leave much for extras. Smith stated that Cantillon mentioned that each workman needed to earn at least double the staple wage, in order to account for children and a wife to care for those children. The mortality rate was relatively high at the time of that writing, related by "one-half the children born, it is computed, die before the age of manhood" (p. 96). The ratio of children equaled "the necessary maintenance of four children, it is supposed, may be nearly equal to that of one man" (p. 96). If the wife could hold out her own labor to not tax the family situation for subsistence, then a workman was compelled to raise four children, losing half before maturation, just to replace the worker population. Another way to state this is that it is the natural rate of wages for the worker or laborer population. Unfortunately for the worker families, this meant that the worker families did not see much of an improvement in their respective lots, even though the economy improved due to the fact that all of this labor, just to subsist, augmented the produce of the economy in general and fostered economic growth in particular (p. 96). Apparently, the economic growth fostered wages higher than just subsistence for the labor population (in order to maintain that population), but not higher wealth for the families involved.

Social Accounts

The productivity of certain national or personal accounts was related back to the use of capital. Smith (1776, 2003) determined the difference between the gross and net product, or the remaining capital, when he stated that, "the value of...annual produce...from the ground, or...productive labourers [sic], is destined not only for replacing a capital, but such a capital as the owner does not care to be at the trouble of employing himself" (p. 364). This related two concepts with regard to macroeconomics. The first was that there was a difference between gross and net production in that the net production, or net capital, was what remained after the workers and producers had subtracted subsistence expenses and the wealth that was needed to be employed for immediate circulation (p. 364). Also, Smith accounted for national wealth by adding together the manufacturer's production and the agricultural production (p. 449). Ricardo (1817, 2004) addressed this set of concepts, which was unheard of as a conceptual relationship (by his own admission) for that time period. Ricardo agreed with Smith and stated that, "The farmer and manufacturer can no more live without profit than the labourer [sic] without wages" (p. 73). Smith realized that the labor involved with agricultural production was higher in productivity than that used in manufacturing, when he included the two types of production together in capital determination for social accounts (p. 847).

Larger concepts were determined by Smith (1776, 2003) when he decided to use rent as a determinant for economic outlook. He noted that rent was an optimal guide for such policies when it was considered that, "Gross revenue is the whole annual produce: net revenue what is left free after deducting the maintenance of fixed and circulating capital" (p. 364). The two main assumptions that buttressed this viewpoint were that plentiful labor would renew itself, at even the basic wages of sustenance, and that the amount of interest, related to the surplus capital loaned at interest, did not matter (p. 365).

The inter-relationship of the three principles was ultimately tied together into one neat concept. Smith (1776, 2003) concluded that there was an important relationship between wages, profits, and rent, and that aggregate price was a function of these three. He maintained that, "the price of the whole annual produce resolves itself into wages, profits and rent" (p. 74). Further, Smith deduced that the surplus, which was the net, was actually what was required to replace capital and thus keep capital in place. He mentioned that capital divided itself into two parts and that, "the largest, is, in the first place, destined for replacing a capital, or for renewing the provisions, materials, and finished work, which had been withdrawn from a capital" (p. 424).

Although the market could reduce the labor wages to basic subsistence levels, as discussed above, there was a more important concept with relation to labor and the associated income. Smith (1776, 2003) decided that as a nation's economic growth and eventual wealth began to increase, a natural by-product was the increase in the demand for "those who live by wages" (p. 98). As previously mentioned, with regard to the replacement of human laborers viewed as economic capital, the actual gross of that income derived from labor could be construed as what was required to keep, at proper maintenance levels, the labor supply in the work-force (p. 98).

Social class was a constituent part of this particular time period and economists were not immune, as evidenced by their writing. Smith (1776, 2003) was a product of his times and he determined that society was composed of three separate and distinct parts when he stated:

> The whole annual produce of the land and labour [sic] of every country, or what comes to the same thing, the whole price of that annual produce, naturally divides itself, it has already been observed, into three parts; the rent of the land, the wages of labour [sic], and the profits of stock; and constitutes a revenue to three different orders of people; to those who live by rent, to those who live by wages, and to those who live by profit. These are the three great, original and constituent orders of every civilized society, from whose revenues that of every other order is ultimately derived. (p. 336)

This social accounting depicted the three orders, or the three basic social accounts, of society in general during that time period and this concept was later to become one of the important planks, taken for granted, in the theoretical platform of classical economics. (Schumpeter 1934, 1961)

Classical Economic School Summary

Smith noted that an individual acted in the best interests of the public by engaging in personal self-interest. Smith specifically stated that individuals were led by an invisible hand to promote an end which was no part of their intention. Since the invisible hand was guiding individuals who then contributed to the overall market's value, this competition among individuals was the practical realization of the invisible hand, or competition, which was what optimized a market's overall performance. Smith reasoned that this self-optimization eventually resulted in market optimization and that this market optimization was good for society.

Smith explained that there were three distinct obligations owed by a government to its citizens: to create and maintain a standing army for national defense; to pay for and maintain a judicial system and; to be responsible for the maintenance, and the original construction, of the civil works and institutions for use by the public because of the prohibitive expense to an individual or group of individuals. Mercantile policy had an impact upon the use of trade. Smith insisted that nothing, however, could be more absurd than this whole doctrine of the balance of trade, upon which, not only these restraints, but almost all the other regulations of commerce were founded. Smith enlarged upon this concept with the idea that, if a foreign country could supply us with a commodity cheaper than we ourselves could make it, we would be better off to buy it from them with some part of the produce employed in a way in which we have some advantage. Ricardo referred to this as the law of comparative advantage, resulting from internal workings of specialization, and Samuelson said that this simple principle provided the unshakable basis for international trade.

Smith explained that rent was the remainder from the complete payment of the expenses to make it possible to cultivate produce. Improvements to the land were a productive expense, which did not relate to the ground expense, and rent in general had to do with land scarcity. Unfortunately, Smith simply was unable to reconcile the relationship between rent and price. Ricardo grasped the significance of this relationship and had some intuitive grasp of the fact that real economic production was related to the land rents and it either directly, or indirectly, related the notional value of rent to price. This nullified Smith's idea that per acre rent to the landlord should rise as a proportion of, or as a function of, superior acreage output. Samuelson explained the land and rent connection very efficiently when he noted that, the price of using a piece of land for a period of time was called its rent. Rent was exactly just a function of time, and had absolutely nothing to do with the output of the land (described by Smith). Samuelson made the allusion that, rent was the payment for the use of the factors of production that were fixed in supply. This was extrapolated from land to all fixed factors of production and became an important foundational issue of macroeconomics.

There was a connection between capital and profit. Smith described that the capital of an individual could only be increased by what that individual saved, so the capital of a society, which was the same as all of the individuals who composed it, could only be increased in the same manner. Smith connected output, rent, capital, and profit. Savings, as capital, could also be loaned at interest. Thus, capital could be increased by savings from profit, savings could eventually become equal to investment or it could be loaned to producers at a given rate of interest. Smith explained that an increase in capital could eventually cause profits to diminish, because there soon were just not enough places to invest that capital. However, even though interest rates fell as the quantity of stock increased, the liquidity movement of that capital, due to increased competition for it, could equalize the rates of that profit among different sectors of industry. Smith felt that profit earners had no interest in the general welfare of the economy, therefore, those who worked for the public trust (politicians) should not be chosen from the profit earner group, because they did not hold with the general interests of the public and were self-serving.

Smith realized that monopolists skewed the allocation of the factors of production by purposely providing the markets with a lower supply than what the market demanded. Smith further observed that the natural price would directly vary with the component parts of the natural price, which were wages, profit, and rent. Smith concluded that the natural price of a commodity was indicative of its composite parts, and was really an aggregate composition of wages, profit, and rent. Another way of stating this was that land, labor, and capital were related to natural price. This concept became a standard, theoretical plank in the platform of classical economics. A further notion of classical economics was that, with regard to skewed pricing, commodities for production were removed if the natural price exceeded the market price.

Smith noted if the supply of the commodity in question was greater than the effectual demand, then the commodity's market price would be lower than the normal price usually obtained; if the supply of the commodity in question was less than the effectual demand, then the commodity's market price would be higher than the normal price usually obtained. So, the amount of the difference would then depend upon the nature of the demand. This relationship, advanced by Smith above and further discussed by Ricardo, was further elaborated upon by Marshall as very plainly, supply and demand. Marshall further discussed the more advanced notion of the elasticity of demand, predicated upon the commodity's supply, which has become another important plank in the classical economic theoretical platform.

Economic growth could be tied to output. Smith realized that one, unskilled workman laboring to produce an item would not contribute greatly to the economy. Smith extrapolated this concept to all employments and all trades, and stated that the division of labor would dramatically increase productivity for any trade or employment. Smith stated that the market would be adversely affected by any and all market restrictions and would eventually have the tendency to decrease economic productivity. Smith deduced that the increasing specialization of the labor force would consequently require an increased application of capital, and the production advantages from that labor specialization would eventually lead to greater scaled returns. Smith realized that there were two reasons for the increased productivity: first, diversity of employment, with regard to labor, would dramatically make productive additions to the economy and; second, in a static economy, the wages moved toward a basic level that would only support the families of workmen. Although this was the natural rate of wages for the laborer population, the economic growth only fostered wages higher than just subsistence for the labor population (in order to maintain that population), but not higher wealth for the families involved.

Productivity, of national or personal accounts, was related back to the use of capital. Smith determined the difference between the gross and net product when he stated that the value of annual produce was destined not only for replacing a capital, but such a capital as the owner did not care to be at the trouble of employing himself. This idea related two concepts with regard to macroeconomics: first, net production was what remained after the workers and producers had subtracted subsistence expenses and the wealth that was needed to be employed for immediate circulation and; second, national wealth was manufacturer's production and the agricultural production combined. Smith realized that the labor involved with agricultural production was higher in productivity than that used in manufacturing, when he included the two types of production together in capital determination for social accounts.

Smith decided to use rent as a determinant for economic outlook when it was considered that gross revenue was the whole annual produce; net revenue what was left free after deducting the maintenance of fixed and circulating capital. Smith maintained that the price of the whole annual produce resolved itself into wages, profits, and rent, and he deduced that the surplus, which was the net, was actually what was required to replace capital and thus keep capital in place. With regard to the replacement of human laborers viewed as economic capital, the actual gross of that income derived from labor could be construed as what was required to keep, at proper maintenance levels, the labor supply in the workforce.

Social class was a constituent part of this particular time period. This social accounting depicted the three orders, or the three basic social accounts from which all other revenue and economic growth flowed, of society in general during that time period. This concept was later to become one of the important planks, taken for granted, in the theoretical platform of classical economics.

John Maynard Keynes and the Keynesian School of Economics

Liquidity Preference

Keynes (1936, 1997) decided that there should be a focus on the actual system, with regard to money, but not a consideration with regard to the bonds that circulated. Keynes felt that "there is a continuous curve relating changes in the demand for money to satisfy the speculative motive and changes in the rate of interest as given by changes in the prices of bonds and debts of various maturities" (p. 197). Samuelson (1948, 1995) expressed the view, however, that "bonds, can be turned into cash quickly for close to their current value" (p. 483). Where Keynes focused upon money, instead of concentrating on the bonds, he was attracted by the lure of the production market and not by the market for assets. Ricardo (1817, 2004) noted that whether, cash, bills or specie were used for a trade that was inherently agreeable to all parties, that it "would exactly produce the same effects" (p. 151). This concept implied something different from what Keynes had thought; it implied that an asset that was missing from a functional demand system could in essence be determined from the remainder of that system.

Keynes (1936, 1997) was very specific about his definitions, when he stated that "Liquidity-preference is a potentiality or functional tendency, which fixes the quantity of money which the public will hold when the rate of interest is given." Keynes qualified this definition with a major assumption stating that there were only two parts to interest: part of interest was attributable to default risk and part of interest was attributable to the future uncertainty of the interest rates that could be attributable to long-term investments (p. 168).

Hicks (1939, 1991) enlarged upon this view of liquidity-preference when he referred to this view by stating that, "to say that the rate of interest on perfectly safe securities is determined by nothing else but uncertainty of future interest rates seems to leave interest hanging by its own boot-straps" (p. 164). Evidently, he noted a considerable exception to the stated principle. He further noted that the cash balances relied upon surpluses determined by income, and that this was positively related to that income and was not related to interest (p. 164). Hicks went on to observe that the trouble associated with investment was what determined the actual liquidity-preference, and that this trouble was what determined the rate of interest as well (p. 165).

Hicks (1939, 1991) noted that Keynes understood that the rate of interest was "determined by the supply and demand for money itself? This last view is put forward by Mr. Keynes in his *General Theory*" (p. 153). Hicks also realized that the interest rate in question was not to be regarded as an item in "isolation." He realized that there was a small chance that a downward movement in the interest rate could cause a dramatic shift to cash, but that this was indeed an exception and the chance possibility of a money trap was distant indeed (p. 154).

Similar to Keynes, Hicks realized that factors involved with supply and demand, with regard to both output and money, together lead to the productive output in general and the interest rates in particular (p. 158). As a working solution to a number of these issues with Keynes' arguments, Hicks proposed the chart solution of the IS/LM curve. This representation put the individual components into a better perspective and related them for a visual representation that was more palatable than what Keynes had proposed (p. 110).

Futility of Wage Reductions

Keynes (1936, 1997) held that classical economists (such as Adam Smith) felt that "real wages are always equal to the marginal disutility of labour [sic] and that the latter increases when employment increases, so that the labour [sic] supply will fall off" (p. 284). He further held, according to his rendition of the same classical economic argument, that when real wages decreased, all things being equal, that there would be no means of promoting further spending with regard to "wage-units." Therefore, Keynes disagreed with classical economists because Keynes stated that, under these special conditions, there would be no means of instituting the "elasticity of employment." Further, employment would not increase in light of higher volumes of money being spent to remedy the situation. This occurred, because "money-wages" would "rise proportionally to the increased money expenditure...consequently no increase in employment" (p. 284). Keynes held, contrary to the classical economic, theoretical position, that "full employment" could only occur when the amount of real wages had dropped far enough to equal labor disutility (p. 284).

Hicks (1939, 1991) mentioned that Pigou had critically devalued Keynes on the previous theoretical discussion described above, due to the fact that the balances of cash increased and this had occurred secondary to the decreased wages, so that economic output then increased and rates of interest dropped (p. 335). This unique phenomenon was explained in great detail by Keynes. This particular phenomenon was later put by Samuelson (1948, 1995) into common usage, in the economic community with his textbook, and it came to be known as the "Pigou Effect" (p. 445).

Keynes (1936, 1997) observed that it was possible to defer, or even eliminate, simultaneous reductions in economic output and employment if the cash balances, in the previous example, had been set into place by monetary increases in supply. The reverse would have occurred, possibly leading to a collapse, if there had been dramatic decreases in wages (pp. 286-287). Hicks

(1939, 1991) held that this sort of thinking, as espoused for example by Keynes, was tantamount to setting the field of economics backward, with regard to theoretical advancement, from dynamics theory, backward in time and complexity to static theory (p. 115).

Stabilization Policy

The tenets of the Keynesian school were very distinct in some respects, with regard to some aspects of stabilization policy theory, but they were circumspect in others. Keynes (1936, 1997) mentioned that an economy, categorized as industrial in nature, was in some form or another, the subject of wage policy. He specifically stated that "to suppose that a flexible wage policy is a right and proper adjunct of a system which on the whole is one of *laissez-faire*, is the opposite of the truth" (p. 269). This is an obvious indictment of the classical school of economics and Adam Smith's views on the economy. Keynes then advanced the view that, in order to curtail any advancement of economic stagnation, a government must immediately institute "sudden, substantial, all-round changes" in order to regulate wages and wage policy. He further noted that this would only be possible in "authoritarian" governments, but would not be enforceable in free-world countries. From Keynes' discussion of investment, wages, output, and employment, it is plain to observe how and when the prototypical plank in the Keynesian school of economics platform was created, with regard to fiscal management of government policy, central planning, and the regulation of demand (p. 269).

Keynes (1936, 1997) refuted all of classical economic theory, and the views of Adam Smith, by stating that "its tacit assumptions are seldom or never satisfied, with the result that it cannot solve the economic problems of the actual world." Keynes mandated that the real solution to a nation's economic problems was through government central planning, with regard to demand. He felt that private ownership of the means of production was acceptable, but that the government should regulate and plan for how those factors should be utilized through central demand planning. He somehow felt that even in a capitalist society, or what is generally known to be a free society, that this would not prove to be an issue when he stated that "the necessary measures of socialisation [sic] can be introduced gradually and without a break in the general traditions of society" (p. 378). Keynes felt that this was how to foster "full employment," and that it was fiscal policy that was the ultimate answer to the economic ills of society; not monetary policy through a central bank (p. 378). As troubling as this line of thought might be to an individual's notional concept of free enterprise and the freedom to pursue competitive economics, as espoused by the classical school of economics, Schumpeter (1942, 2008) observed that this sort of Keynesian type of finance, or functioning finance, was later espoused and promulgated as demand planning fiscal policy by Abba Lerner, along with some rather detailed, intricate additions and refinements (p. 176).

Wage Rigidity

There were some differences between classical and Keynesian theory. Keynes (1936, 1997) realized that classical theory was based upon the assumption that "money-wages" were somewhat fluid and that this "fluidity" caused the automatically "self-adjusting" nature of the "economic system" at large. He felt that wage rigidity was a basic assumption of his system, and why it had a tendency to be functional, whereas this sort of wage rigidity was the downfall of the auto-correcting mechanism closely associated with the classical economics, economic system. Keynes' response to the problems associated with "maladjustment" was to decrease the price of finished goods down to where "money-wages is just offset by the diminishing marginal efficiency of labour [sic] as output (from a given equipment) is increased" (p. 257). He reasoned that since the unemployed, as a group, were in existence due to wage inflexibility, that the overall concepts of unemployment and rigid wages were just lack of adjustment issues (p. 257).

Keynes (1936, 1997) felt that the adjustment of wages, as a function of rigidity, would lead to full employment given the concept of equilibrium as a foundational precursor. So, complete employment and total adjustment of wages were characteristics of economic, stationary equilibrium (p. 257). However, this did not seem to crystallize into economic reality, since Hicks (1939, 1991) explicitly stated that, "No economic system ever does exhibit perfect equilibrium over time; nevertheless the ideal is approached more nearly at some times than at others" (p. 133). Although stationary equilibrium seemed integral to the above tenet of Keynesian theory, Hicks clearly stated that Keynes' scenario, as described in detail by Keynes, probably did not occur very often in the real world (p. 133).

The Multiplier

The Keynesian School of Economics detailed a situation that was described by a certain numbered ratio, with regard to economic factors. Keynes (1936, 1997) credited Kahn (Keynes noted that Kahn described this concept in a 1931 article) with the introduction of such a ratio that had been placed into common usage, in the field of economics, known as *the multiplier*. Keynes determined that "between income and investment and, subject to certain simplifications, between the total employment and the employment directly employed on investment," that there was a certain multiplier that was in an exact proportional relationship to the "propensity to consume" (p. 113). This multiplier improved circumstances beyond Keynes' idea of unity, or a ratio or a factor of 1:1, and basically translated those circumstances into multiple dollars of increased income, for an economy, for every dollar that was economically invested beyond economic output equilibrium (p. 113).

Keynesian theory also described the effects of public works and employment, with regard to the multiplier, concerning investment and the consumer psychology. Keynes (1936, 1997) found that, for example, if a particular community's predisposition was to consume ninety-percent of "an increment of income," then the multiplier then became a factor of 10 and employment fostered by improved spending on public works would also improve "primary employment" by the same factor of 10, if money was not diverted to other uses and all things were kept equal in that specific situation. Therefore, in this particular situation, the investment in public works, in that specific community, improved job creation ten-fold (pp. 116-117). Hicks (1939, 1991) related that this sort of static theory, as depicted in this Keynesian multiplier example, "gives one's static theory some slight dynamic flavouring [sic], it can be made to look much more directly applicable to the real world" (p. 115).

Effective Demand

Keynes (1936, 1997), on the subject of *effective demand*, agreed with the classical economists (Marshall 1923, 2003; Ricardo 1817, 2004; Smith 1776, 2003) in theory and in spirit, but not in practice. Keynes rightly stated that the classical economists believed that supply and demand were both related in that the equalization point moved along a graphed function so that there were points where demand equaled supply, up to the point where labor disutility became problematic and the economic output diminished and foundered. In practice, since in the Keynesian school of economic thought supply did not create its own demand, there was only *one* equilibrium point where supply equaled demand. Therefore, "effective demand" had a particular "equilibrium value." The really big difference between the two schools of economic thought was that Keynes differed from the classical, implied, full employment assumption in that he thought that there was a model extant that would describe a situation that amounted to unemployment numbers that would coexist with equilibrium demand and supply (pp. 25-26).

Samuelson (1948, 1995) discussed this corollary, to the Keynesian theorem of a static equilibrium point with regard to supply and demand, when he mentioned that classical economics mandated that, with certain assumptions, as the accepted propensity to invest increased the capital stock, the capital's efficiency declined to the current rate of interest. This was synonymous with Fisher's "competitive rate of return." To Samuelson, this meant two very important things: "It rations out society's scarce supply of capital goods for uses that have the highest rates of return, and it induces people to sacrifice current consumption in order to increase the stock of capital" (p. 251). Efficient use of scarce resources and the sacrifice of current consumption for future needs became important contributions to basic, macroeconomic theory (p. 251).

Keynesian Economic School Summary

Keynes decided that there should be a focus on the actual system, with regard to money, but not a consideration with regard to the bonds that circulated. Samuelson expressed the view that bonds could be turned into cash quickly for close to their current value. Where Keynes focused upon money, instead of concentrating on the bonds, he was attracted by the lure of the production market and not by the market for assets. Ricardo noted that cash, bills or specie used for trade would exactly produce the same effects. This implied something different from what Keynes had thought; that an asset that was missing from a functional demand system could in essence be determined from the remainder of that system.

Keynes stated that there were only two parts to interest: part of interest was attributable to default risk and part of interest was attributable to the future uncertainty of the interest rates that could be attributable to long-term investments. Hicks enlarged upon this view by stating that, if the rates of interest on perfectly safe securities were determined by nothing else but uncertainty of future interest rates, this left interest hanging by its own boot-straps. He further noted that cash balances relied upon surpluses determined by income, and that this was positively related to that income and was not related to interest. Hicks went on to observe that the trouble associated with investment, was what determined the actual liquidity-preference, and that this trouble was what determined the rate of interest as well.

Hicks noted that Keynes understood that the rate of interest was determined by the supply and demand for money itself, but that there was a small chance that a downward movement in the interest rate could cause a shift to cash, or a liquidity trap, but that this was indeed an exception and the chance possibility of this occurring was distant indeed. Keynes and Hicks realized that factors involved with supply and demand, with regard to both output and money, together lead to the productive output in general and the interest rates in particular. As a working solution for the weakness of some of Keynes' arguments, Hicks proposed the chart solution of the IS/LM curve, which was a representation that put the individual components into better perspective graphically, and related them for a visual representation that was more palatable than what Keynes had originally proposed.

Keynes held that classical economists felt that real wages were always equal to the marginal disutility of labor, and that the disutility increased when employment increased, so that the labor supply would decrease. Therefore, Keynes disagreed with classical economists because Keynes stated that, under these special conditions, there would be no means of instituting the elasticity of employment. Keynes held (contrary to the classical economic position), that full employment could only occur when the amount of real wages had dropped far enough to equal labor disutility. Hicks mentioned that Pigou had critically devalued Keynes' views on this idea, due to the fact that the balances of cash increased and this had occurred secondary to the decreased wages, so that economic output then increased and the rates of interest dropped. This unique phenomenon was explained in great detail by Keynes and, later, Samuelson put it into common usage in the economic community with his text and it came to be known as the Pigou Effect.

Keynes observed that it was possible to defer, or even eliminate, simultaneous reductions in economic output and employment if the cash balances, in the previous example, had been set into place by monetary increases in supply. The reverse would have occurred, possibly leading to a collapse, if there had been dramatic decreases in wages. Hicks held that this sort of thinking, as espoused for example by Keynes, was tantamount to setting the field of economics backward, with regard to theoretical advancement, from dynamics theory backward in time and complexity to static theory.

Keynes stated that to suppose that a flexible wage policy was a right and proper adjunct of a system, which on the whole was one of *laissez-faire*, was the opposite of the truth. This was an obvious indictment of the classical school of economics and Adam Smith's views on the economy. Keynes advanced the view that, in order to curtail any advancement of economic stagnation, a government must immediately institute sudden, substantial, all-round changes in order to regulate wages and wage policy. He further noted that this would only be possible in "authoritarian" governments, but would not be enforceable in free-world countries. From Keynes' discussion of investment, wages, output, and employment, it is plain to observe how and when this prototypical plank in the Keynesian school of economics platform was created, with regard to government policy, central planning, and the system-wide regulation of demand.

Keynes refuted all of classical economic theory, and the views of Adam Smith, when he stated that its tacit assumptions were seldom or never satisfied, with the result that it cannot solve the economic problems of the actual world. Keynes mandated that the real solution to a nation's economic problems was through government central planning, with regard to demand. He felt that even in a capitalist society, or what was generally known to be a free society, that this demand planning would not prove to be an issue when he stated that the necessary measures of socialization could be introduced gradually and without a break in the general traditions of society. Keynes felt that this was how to foster full employment, and that it was fiscal policy that was the ultimate answer to the economic ills of society; not monetary policy. Schumpeter observed that this sort of Keynesian type of finance, or functioning finance, was later espoused by Abba Lerner, along with some rather detailed, intricate additions and refinements, and became the basis for central government fiscal policy and system-wide demand planning.

Keynes realized that classical theory was based upon the assumption that money-wages were somewhat fluid and that this fluidity caused the automatically self-adjusting nature of the economic system at large. He felt that wage rigidity was a basic assumption of his system, and why it had a tendency to be functional, whereas this sort of wage rigidity was the downfall of the auto-correcting mechanism closely associated with the classical economics, economic system. Keynes' response to these problems was to decrease the price of finished goods down to where money-wages were just offset by the diminishing marginal efficiency of labor, as output was increased. He reasoned that since the unemployed, as a group, were in existence due to wage inflexibility, that the overall concepts of unemployment and rigid wages were just lack of adjustment issues.

Keynes felt that the adjustment of wages, as a function of rigidity, would lead to full employment given the concept of equilibrium as a foundational precursor. Complete employment and total adjustment of wages were characteristics of economic, stationary equilibrium.

But, this did not seem to crystallize into economic reality. Although stationary equilibrium seemed integral to the above tenet of Keynesian theory, Hicks clearly stated that Keynes' scenario, as described in detail by Keynes, probably did not occur very often in the real world.

Keynes credited Kahn with the introduction of such a ratio that had been placed into common usage, in the field of economics, known as the multiplier. Keynes determined that between income and investment and, subject to certain simplifications, between the total employment and the employment directly employed on investment, that there was a certain multiplier that was in an exact proportional relationship to the propensity to consume. This multiplier improved for an economy, for every dollar that was economically invested beyond economic output equilibrium. Keynesian theory also described the effects of public works and employment, with regard to the multiplier, concerning investment and the consumer psychology. Keynes found that if a particular community's predisposition was to consume ninety-percent of an increment of income, then the multiplier then became a factor of 10 and employment fostered by improved spending on public works would also improve primary employment by the same factor of 10 (if money was not diverted to other uses and all things were kept equal in that specific situation). Investment in public works, in that specific community, improved job creation ten-fold. Hicks related that this sort of static theory, as depicted in this Keynesian multiplier example, gave one's static theory some slight dynamic flavoring so that it could be made to look much more directly applicable to the real world.

Keynes stated that classical economists believed that supply and demand were both related in that the equalization point moved along a graphed function so that there were points where demand equaled supply, up to the point where labor disutility became problematic and the economic output diminished and foundered. The Keynesian school of economic thought differed with the notion that supply did not create its own demand, and that there was only *one* equilibrium point where supply equaled demand. Therefore, effective demand had a particular equilibrium value. The Keynesian school differed from the classical, implied, full employment assumption in that Keynesians thought that there was a model extant that would describe a situation that amounted to unemployment numbers that would coexist with equilibrium demand and supply.

Samuelson discussed this corollary, to the Keynesian theorem of a static equilibrium point with regard to supply and demand, when he mentioned that classical economics mandated, with certain assumptions, as the accepted propensity to invest increased the capital stock, that the capital's efficiency declined to the current rate of interest. This was synonymous with Fisher's competitive rate of return. To Samuelson, this meant two very important things: it rationed out society's scarce supply of capital goods for uses that have the highest rates of return, and it induced people to sacrifice current consumption, in order to increase the stock of capital.

Milton Friedman and the Monetarist School of Economics

Income permanence as the pre-cursor to rational expectations

Samuelson (1948, 1995) defined "modern monetary economics" as the school of thought in the field of economics, or "monetarism" as it eventually became known in common parlance, as that particular school of economic thought that was principally "developed after World War II by Chicago's Milton Friedman" (p. 607). Shortly before the U.S. entered World War II, Hicks (1939, 1991) stated that he agreed with the Keynesian approach (in theory, but not in particular) that explained that personal income was a function, *ex ante*, of aggregate income, *ex post*, in that the *ex post* income was actually the addition of a "windfall gain to any of our preceding definitions of income (or subtract the loss), we get a new set of definitions, definitions of 'income including windfalls' or 'income *ex post*' " (p. 178). In other words, Hicks felt that if the equation were bereft of transitory factors arising from human capital's cumulative efforts, then the aggregate, or permanent income, was to be viewed as objective, versus subjective (p. 178).

Thus, the propensity to consume would not decrease with rising income, which was a concept contrary to the definition given by Keynes (Keynes 1936, 1997). Friedman (1953) further enlarged upon that concept with the notion that the *ex post* income described above by Hicks, would *be* the permanent income and that final income would not be related to any transient income, and that the transient income factors would not be related to one another. Friedman stated that Marshall described the component parts to this concept as, since real income was unaffected, one commodity substituted for another and that this idea became known as the "substitution effect." Also, when price declined so that consumer wealth increased (but money income was unaltered), this became known as the "income effect" (p. 64). Hicks (1939, 1991) brought in the notion of "inconsistent expectations" (p. 178) and it was eventually tied, in retrospect, by Samuelson

(1948, 1995) to "rational expectations," which did far more than imply that, "because of rational expectations the government cannot fool the people with systematic economic policies" (p. 612). This essentially meant that if the public had a better understanding of economics and economic policies, that the government would not be able to goad the public into agreeing to some of the extant fiscal policies of central demand planning.

Comparisons of Keynesian economics, classical economics and monetarism

Samuelson (1948, 1995) held that "Keynesian theories hold that many different forces affect aggregate demand, monetarists argue that changes in the money supply are the primary factor that determines output and price movements." He held the view that monetarist philosophy dictated that the actual supply of money in the economy prompted short term changes in the "nominal GDP" and that the money supply was the cause of price changes over the "long-run" (p. 605). The real, tangible result of monetarism was the belief that the use of monetary policy could be used to reduce the likelihood of a recession. If the management of the money supply could be used to reduce the possibility of a recession, and recessions eventually lead to a depression, then the implications of this concept were enormous with regard to the potential elimination of millions of dollars lost and the psycho-social implications and impacts brought on by depressions in general. This implied that the use of monetarism, through the use of monetary policy, could in theory be used to stave off a depression (p. 559).

Samuelson (1948, 1995) concluded that there were three principal tenets to monetarism and how it related to other schools of economic thought. He mentioned that "monetarism, like Keynesian multiplier theory, is basically a theory of the determinants of aggregate demand" (p. 607). To contrast this, Samuelson stated Friedman's two principal assumptions were that, in relation to the monetarist's view of the "primacy of money," that the stability of the velocity of income would impress any fiscal technician and that "the demand for money is completely insensitive to interest rates" (p. 607). The first reason for the rationale of why these two principal assumptions conclusively lead to the monetarist view of *Economics*, was that with a stable velocity of money, there was no means of contention allowed from the government or taxes because the supply of money would conclusively determine "nominal GDP." The second of three reasons was that, since the Keynesian school viewed wages and prices to be "sticky," the monetarists assumed that "(1) money is the prime determinant of nominal GDP and

(2) prices and wages are fairly flexible around potential output, the implication is that money moves real output only modestly and for a short time. M mainly affects P" (p. 607). But since the supply of money had an impact on prices and even output during the "short-run," if the tendency was toward "full employment," then the real impact for the long run was the economy's "price level." Monetarism agreed, in principle, with classical economics on the third and final point. Monetarism believed that *"the private sector is stable."* Much of economic policy had to do with the fiscal policies put into place by the government and the monetary policies put into place by the central bank of the country. Since the private sector was not predisposed to instability, if left to its own devices, the economy would be just fine (p. 608). Monetarism refuted the government's position that there was a need to manage the economy with central demand planning through the use of fiscal policy.

Friedman's views on banking and the supply of money

Friedman and Schwartz (1963, 1993) expressed significant concerns over the fractional banking system put in place by the Federal Reserve Bank of the United States. Friedman had concerns over the stability of the fractional system of banking in general, advocated by the Federal Reserve, and their continued policies for the advocacy of the reduction of reserve requirements along with the concomitant risks of instability implied by those reduced reserve requirements. He was somewhat relieved when the Board passed a measure in the early 1940's to improve the reserve requirements, as a fraction of outstanding debt, to purportedly increase monetary stability in the economy. This rise in the ratios, prompted by the Board, was indeed, however, short-lived (p. 556).

Friedman and Schwartz (1963, 1993) contended that the creation of the Federal Reserve, initially, had helped the government and the nation to spread more money around the economy than would have otherwise been possible. This was an extraordinarily large help to help stem the tide of inflation after the First World War. However, it did not seem to have lasted the duration (p. 219). This Federal Reserve toll on the economy at large, however, seemed to dilute the government's power because of the sharing of the ability to create money, since banks could now do so with the multiplier, and give up its inherent monopoly on debentures, that bore no interest, by sharing with the commercial banks (p. 568). Friedman was uncomfortable with this sharing arrangement and felt that the Reserve Board should replace money that was restricted for use by the banks, through some compensating arrangements for an expansion of the supply of money. This would, in theory, postpone or eliminate fiscal contractions in the economy, because of the replacement to the constricted supply of money, and it would promote stability (p. 569).

Monetarist Economic School Summary

Samuelson defined monetarism as that particular school of economic thought that was developed after World War Two by Chicago's Milton Friedman. Hicks stated that he agreed with the Keynesian approach in that the *ex post* income was actually income including windfalls. In other words, Hicks felt that if the equation were bereft of transitory factors arising from human capital's cumulative efforts, then the aggregate, or permanent income, was to be viewed as objective, versus subjective.

Thus, the propensity to consume would not decrease with rising income, contrary to Keynes, and Friedman further enlarged upon that concept with the notion that the *ex post* income described above by Hicks, would *be* the permanent income and that final income would not be related to any transient income, and that the transient income factors would not be related to one another. Friedman stated that Marshall described one commodity substituted for another and that this idea became known as the substitution effect. Also, when price declined, this became known as the income effect. Hicks brought in the notion of inconsistent expectations and Samuelson tied this to rational expectations, which implied that the government could not fool the people with systematic economic policies. Monetarism refuted the government's position that there was a need to manage the economy with central demand planning through the use of fiscal policy.

Samuelson held that Keynesian theories held that many different forces affected aggregate demand and monetarists argued that changes in the money supply were the primary factor that determined output and price movements. Monetarist philosophy dictated that the actual supply of money, in the economy, prompted short term changes in the nominal GDP, and that the money supply was the cause of price changes over the long-run. The real, tangible result of monetarism was the belief that the use of monetarism, through the use of monetary policy, could in theory be used to stave off a potential depression.

Samuelson concluded that there were three principal tenets to monetarism and how it related to other schools of economic thought. Monetarism, like the Keynesian multiplier theory, was basically a theory of the determinants of aggregate demand. Friedman's two principal assumptions were that, in relation to the monetarist's view of the primacy of money, that the stability of the velocity of income would impress any fiscal technician and that the demand for money was completely insensitive to interest rates. The reason for the rationale of why these two principal assumptions conclusively lead to the monetarist view of economics was that with a stable velocity of money, there was no means of contention allowed from the government or taxes because the supply of money would conclusively determine nominal GDP. The second of three reasons was that, since the Keynesian school viewed wages and prices to be 'sticky,' the monetarists assumed that (1) money was the prime determinant of nominal GDP and (2) prices and wages were fairly flexible around potential output. The implication was that money moved real output only modestly and for a short time. Since the supply of money had an impact on prices and even output during the short-run, if the tendency was toward full employment, then the real impact for the long run was the economy's price level. Monetarism agreed with classical economics on the third and final point. Monetarism believed that the private sector was stable. Since so much of economic policy had to do with the fiscal policies put into place by the government, and the monetary policies put into place by the central bank of the country, since the private sector was not predisposed to instability, if left to its own devices, the economy would be just fine.

Friedman had concerns over the stability of the fractional system of banking in general, advocated by the Federal Reserve, and their continued policies for the advocacy of the reduction of reserve requirements along with the concomitant risks of instability implied by those reduced reserve requirements. Friedman contended that the creation of the Federal Reserve, initially, helped the government and the nation to spread more money around the economy than would have otherwise been possible, and that this was a large help to help stem the tide of inflation after the First World War. This Federal Reserve toll on the economy at large, however, seemed to dilute the government's power because of the sharing of the ability to create money, since banks could now do so with the multiplier. The government gave up its inherent monopoly on debentures that bore no interest, by sharing with the commercial banks. Friedman felt that the Reserve Board should replace money that was restricted for use by the banks, through some compensating arrangements for an expansion of the supply of money and that this would, in theory, postpone or eliminate fiscal contractions in the economy. The replacement of the constricted supply of money promoted economic stability. Although many monetarist views have been used by the Federal Reserve, fractional reserve continues to be in use and the leverage ratio continues to increase. Hopefully, Friedman's concerns will not be realized, and this Federal Reserve practice will not eventually de-stabilize the economy.

Breadth Summary

The Breadth component of this KAM demonstration compared and contrasted the synthesis of economic thought of the three primary economic schools of macroeconomic theory: Adam Smith as the primary theorist of the classicist school; John Maynard Keynes as the primary theorist of the Keynesian school; and Milton Friedman as the primary theorist of the monetarist school (Chicago School of Economics). Several concepts of the platform of the classicist school of macroeconomics discussed were the: Invisible Hand; liberalism and mercantilism; land and rent; capital and profit; price; labor and wages; and social accounts. These concepts are integral to the understanding of the classicist school of economic thought and are the basis for further discussion in other segments of this paper. Several concepts of the platform of the Keynesian school of macroeconomics discussed were the: liquidity preference; futility of wage reductions; stabilization policy; wage rigidity; the multiplier; and effective demand. These concepts are integral to the understanding of the Keynesian school of economic thought and are the basis for further discussion in other segments of this paper. Several concepts of the platform of the monetarist school of macroeconomics discussed were the: income permanence as the precursor to rational expectations; comparisons of Keynesian Economics, classical Economics and Monetarism; and Friedman's views on banking and the supply of money. These concepts are integral to the understanding of the monetarist school of economic thought and are the basis for further discussion in other segments of this paper. Several minor theorists, who expounded upon these schools of thought and how those enhancements contributed to the three basic theorists' work, were also analyzed to communicate their contributions to the development of macroeconomics theory.

Each of the three principal schools of macroeconomic schools of thought were summarized, analyzed, and contrasted throughout this Breadth segment and were synthesized into a comparison and contrast of thought in the monetarist portion of the Breadth segment. The demonstration evaluated the strengths and limitations of the tenets of macroeconomics theory, as espoused by the principal macroeconomics theorists Smith, Keynes, and Friedman and enlarged upon by the minor theorists, for the purpose of establishing how their cumulative, theoretical work has contributed to the development of macroeconomics and to the development of a platform of values that is useful in applied macroeconomics as it relates to economic computer modeling and economic forecasting.

Depth

Current Research In Macroeconomics

Annotated Bibliography

Campbell, J., & Krane, S. (2005). Consumption-based macroeconomic forecasting. *Economic Perspectives, 29*(4), 52-70. Accession Number: 19121456, 2008, from Business Source Premier database.

Campbell and Krane (2005) explained how those who make policy and conduct research use macroeconomic models to predict, or forecast, the economy's macroeconomic aggregates. The authors stated that the econometric models were usually so large, that a number of restrictions had to be placed upon those models to make them useful. However, the greater the number of restrictions utilized, the less useful they contended that the models became, because the total aggregates were skewed too far from a realistic depiction of the actual parts of the economy examined. The authors claimed to have solved this issue by taking a smaller slice of the economy, with regard to the macroeconomic aggregates used for attempted forecasting, and that they had placed fewer restrictions on those data and the models in question. Their goal was to pick just a few factors, build a much smaller model and arrive at some conclusions that would be useful for those who made policy and conducted research, to be able to use those macroeconomic models to predict and forecast with the use of "a small-scale econometric model designed to separate the influence of permanent and transitory factors on the level of economic activity" (p. 52). They succeeded in doing this with a sample and the use of some statistical methods that showed that their research was not only valuable, but also applicable in the real world.

The research question was well framed and significant and their research was well related to the existing body of knowledge and it was an extension of the body of knowledge surveyed; thus, it made an original contribution to the existing body of knowledge. The researchers used the typical macroeconomic parameters in their theoretical framework: nondurable goods' consumption and the spending of households and varied groups of factors that don't show long-term adjustments. They used a monetarist model of assumptions for their small, econometric forecasting model. The theoretical framework for the study was adequate and appropriate and the researchers communicated clearly and fully; however their mathematics were a little convoluted.

Their research method was appropriate and there was a sufficient sample size, even though their time period examined was 1983-2005 (instead of going back to the 1960's to include the turbulent economic 1970's as money models sometimes do) so there was probably not a better way of finding the answers to the limited scope of research questions posed. They more than adequately controlled for researcher bias with some stringent limitations to the study, so the research should be replicable with the same data sets. The findings should be generalizable, according to the limits imposed on the study, and in that particular respect, the conclusions were justified by the results of the study.

Chen, S. (2005). Trends in agent-based computational modeling of macroeconomics. *New Generation Computing, 23*(1), 3-11. Accession Number 15621275, 2008, from Academic Search Premier database.

Chen (2005) discussed a considerable amount of trending in the survey of previous and current research in this article that concerned macroeconomic modeling;

over 50 pieces of research previously published as trade articles. Chen was particularly interested in, and discussed at length, "agent engineering" with regard to two particular avenues of research into the modeling associated with computer tools: the work on the periphery of artificial intelligence, and the modeling of behavior and its adaptations, and the framework of the psychological aspect of cognition, when related to affiliated sciences (p. 3). Chen's article was important in that it considered the modeling aspects of the individual agents in a computer forecasting model for macroeconomics. So, this article would be important to those who were interested in the agent factors that influenced the accuracy and applicability of macroeconomic models in forecasting.

Chen (2005) framed a research question that considered a current framework of the "micro-macro" economic computational model that moved beyond neo-classical definitions and parameters. The parametric considerations were beyond the existing body of knowledge and made an original contribution to the existing body of knowledge by extending it (p. 7). The theoretical framework was unique in that it demonstrated how economic research could benefit from "experimental economics" (p. 5). The researcher communicated clearly and fully the results, but this paper was a follow-up to the original study conducted and explained some assumptions made in that original study. Thus, the method was explained, but was used in the original study. The indications were that the sample size was sufficient, and that there were adequate controls for researcher bias.

Without the original study's results for detailed viewing, there was no realistic means of determining whether or not the research was replicable or what the original limitations were of the original study. The findings appear to be generalizable, but the paper was an extended view of the original study - there was no mathematical means evident to determine if the conclusions were justified by the results. However, the thorough nature of the discussion in this trade article would suggest that this could be a reasonable conclusion.

Dabla-Norris, E., & Feltenstein, A. (2005). The underground economy and its macroeconomic consequences. *The Journal of Policy Reform, 8*(2), 153-174. DOI: 10.1080/13841280500086388, 2008, from Academic Search Premier database.

Dabla-Norris and Feltenstein (2005) constructed a model in this study that evaluated performing participants, who circumvented taxes through business conducted in an "underground economy," with the use of a non-static "dynamic general equilibrium" framework. The framework examined the costs to firms, who were constricted in the release of credit from banks, due to the participants who had evaded the taxes levied in that economy. The framework showed a computer depiction of taxes that were levied so high, without the necessary adjustments from the budget regulation to prevent it, that the total investment in the economy was lowered due to higher tax rates that eventually resulted in a minimized base for tax collection. The researchers maintained that minimal taxes would reduce or completely dispose of such an underground economy for business, but that the resulting lack of tax funds would create untenable economic budgets and an eventually deficient trade mechanism. The researchers contended that optimized taxation, with their model, would produce a sufficient amount of funds from a tax base to run an economy, but that this optimized result would inevitably result in some sort of minimal underground business. This research was important in that it addressed a topic that had significance with respect to the use of macroeconomic modeling, with regard to the factors that were generally not officially recognized as part of macroeconomic models (p. 153). This article was valuable in that it fit into place one more part of computational macroeconomic modeling used for forecasting and prediction in an economy.

The research question was well framed and significant, and the research related to the existing body of knowledge by extending that body with original contributions to it. The theoretical framework for the study was adequate and appropriate, and the researchers communicated clearly and fully. The research method was appropriate, but made some peculiar assumptions in order to make the constructed model work, such as ignoring the bureaucratic corruption that may have originally lead to the creation of the underground economy and the view that firms could straddle the economic fence by gleaning the best of both worlds; operating part of their business in the formal, upright economy and part in the underground economy.

There may be a better way to find the answers to the research question, but the narrow assumptions for the model created would have to change, the sample size would have to be larger and the controls for researcher bias would need to change. The research, in its present form, could probably be replicated with the same data set and there were very stringent limitations in this study in order to research the published findings conclusions. The findings are generalizable, but probably only to the third and fourth world countries discussed, and not to free world countries that are more obviously characterized by capitalism, instead of the assumed, mixed model of socialist demand planning and capitalism. The conclusions, in the narrow framework depicted by the study, were justified by the results.

Foote, C. (2007). Space and time in macroeconomic panel data: Young workers and unemployment revisited. *Research Review, 8*, 16-18. Accession Number 31589110, 2008, from Academic Search Premier database. Working paper of the Federal Reserve Bank of Boston, W-07-10. Full text downloaded from http://www.bos.frb.org/economic/wp/wp2007/wp0710.pdf.

Foote (2007) explored a previous study and changed the results, although the actual errors in Foote's study were just as large as in the original study examined. The original study was changed by the use of panel data that extended the original study's period by an additional ten years. Thus, the additional data changed the original study from a negative correlation to a positive correlation, and as the author contended, the new study's results were more appropriate to the data and were "close to what a conventional model would imply." Although the margins for error were still rather large, it was interesting to note how the addition of ten years of data actually changed the results of the original, landmark study, with regard to unemployment and the youthful workers. The time and space attributes of the panel data in the macroeconomic model were critical to the new, updated study and the article was valuable in that it extended the original data with new research, however unreliable the methods were through their use of "regional panel data," instead of national data from a much larger data sample (p. 1).

The research question was well framed and significant because it extended the original study, from 1973 to 1995, to include the years up to 2005. The research was an extended view of the existing body of knowledge, because it extended the original study for an additional ten years of data, to make an original contribution to the existing body of knowledge. The theoretical framework for the study was adequate and appropriate and the researcher communicated clearly and fully the final conclusion that his research changed the results of the original study, with the additional years of data. The researcher added that there were still large gaps due to continued standard error and that the type of regional panel data used was not an optimal predictor of unemployment with relation to young workers as other data might have been.

The research method was appropriate and there might be a better way of finding answers to the research question, if some way were eventually found to ameliorate the effects of the regional panel data, which was unrelated to the sufficiency of the sample size. There were adequate controls for researcher bias and the research, using the same data, should be replicable. The limitations of the study were not the size of the research sample, but the type of data set utilized. The findings are probably generalizable, as stated by the author with regard to the usual use of a conventional macroeconomic model for data forecasting and prediction. The conclusions, when the margins for standard error were addressed with relation to the type of data set utilized in the study, now appear to be justified by the results.

Garner, C. (2005). Consumption taxes: Macroeconomic effects and policy issues. *Economic Review, 90*(2), 5-29. Accession Number 17386035, 2008, from Business Source Premier database.

Garner (2005) addressed the issue of "tax reform," with regard to taxation that could be perceived to be more equitable to the taxpayers in the economic base examined. The researcher presumed that a consumption tax would be more equitable, because such a tax would "increase saving and real output per person over the long run." However, the researcher felt that the overall terminal effects associated with such a reformed tax were indeterminate, based upon the literature survey conducted in the article. From a macroeconomic forecasting model standpoint, the researcher felt that the changes to include such a tax scheme would necessitate considerable "economic adjustments" in the short-run and foster a number of difficulties for the policy determinations associated with fiscal management in the long-run. The article was important with regard to macroeconomic computational modeling. It addressed a concept that many researchers sometimes avoid, in their data types and constraint assumptions, which are conventionally used in more conventional macroeconomic models (p. 5). The value of this article was a direct result of the alternate viewpoint presented by the researcher, who made an important point about tax reform. Intuition informs the most uninitiated, however, that this sort of unconventional tax reform would probably find a difficult way through the legislative organism of big government in contemporary society.

The research question was well framed and significant, and the research related well to the existing body of knowledge by extending that knowledge in an alternate direction. Therefore, it made an original contribution to the existing body of knowledge by providing an alternative solution. The theoretical framework for the study was adequate and appropriate and the researcher communicated clearly and fully. The research method for the comparison of different types of taxes, the foundations for those taxes and their perceived mixed results was appropriate. There might be a better way to find answers to the research questions, but it would probably involve much larger data tables because the sample size seemed sufficient for this study. The controls for researcher bias were adequate and the research for this data set should be replicable. The limitations of the study were the types of taxation examined, with relation to the convoluted present tax structure, and the implications that the effects on the economy were unclear, or indeterminate. The findings appear to be generalizable, and the comment made by the researcher summed up the fact that the conclusions were justified by the results, within the narrow margin of thought with three proposed consumption taxes, in that, "Such consumption taxes can provide greater incentives for working and saving, although they raise a variety of difficult issues, such as their effects on the income distribution and the value of existing assets" (p. 24).

Genberg, H. (2005). The macroeconomic effects of adjustment lending: A review and evaluation. *The Journal of Policy Reform, 8*(1), 1-40. DOI: 10.1080/1384128042000328923, 2008, from Business Source Premier database.

Genberg (2005) described a scenario concerning the effects of external aid on an economy, and the avenues that the proposed aid might follow. Genberg surveyed a number of studies that focused upon the political environment in which "domestic policy" was made, and the researcher specifically focused upon the structure of the correspondence between economic growth and the proposed aid in question. The relationships that were empirically explored in the study were "between aid, government, fiscal responses, private sector investment, and economic growth." The study was important in that it empirically studied the macroeconomics of aid with the relationship to domestic policy and looked at the way that the aid manifested itself in that domestic policy, with regard to the structural framework of policy making (p. 1). The article was valuable in that it empirically modeled the macroeconomic nature of the structure of domestic policy-making and gave the reader an insight into this formulation with respect to the manifestation of aid through the use of economic growth models.

The research covered almost 500 observations, in multiple sets of four year averages, for over 100 countries. The research question was well framed and significant. It was interesting how the researcher related this research to the existing body of knowledge by extending the existing body of knowledge with a comparison of his present findings, using an actual comparison chart with tabulations and results, to the previous findings. The study made an original contribution by extending the knowledge envelope of the previous studies. The theoretical framework for the study was adequate and appropriate and the researcher communicated clearly and fully with detailed explanations and a number of mathematical descriptions. The research method was appropriate. There may be a better way to find answers to the research questions, but it would probably involve a much larger sample size even though the sample used in this study was adequate.

There were adequate controls set in place for researcher bias and the researcher discussed those controls and the accompanying statistical adjustments at length. The research, using the same data sets, should be replicable and the limitations of the study were that it was principally concerned with the countries in sub-Saharan Africa and East Asia. The findings, however, should be generalizable if one were concerned with these issues in third and fourth world countries. In this manner, if this area of the world were being discussed, the conclusions would be justified by the results.

Ghersi, F., & Hourcade, J. (2006). Macroeconomic consistency issues in e3 modeling: The continued fable of the elephant and the rabbit. *The Energy Journal; Hybrid Modeling of Energy-Environme, 27*, 39-61. Accession Number 23914016, 2008, from Business Source Premier.

Ghersi and Hourcade (2006) discussed the constraints of standard "production functions" in a matrix of unconventional relationships, to a framework of the use of those functions that was opposite to the regular trickle down policy framework used in current energy research. The researchers discussed the hypothetical upward philosophy of decision making that was different from the conventionally accepted trickle down approach regularly utilized for such decisions. However, the lines of communication and the possibilities of the trickling down conventionality were employed in conjunction with the theoretical upward policy formulation to help determine the projected, carbon-footprint, energy legacy that we, as world energy stewards, would leave to our progeny in the year 2030. The main result that the researchers were attempting to achieve was a new standard macroeconomic model for energy usage through the use of "bottom-up results" leading to some formalized findings concerning "a significant bias in cost assessment." This study was important because it treated the use of energy in an alternate manner and conceived of the effects that we leave to future generations (p. 39). It was a valuable article in that it explored these actions that we take with daily decisions in a different, unconventional manner to broaden the science of macroeconomic modeling with relation to factors of energy consumption, usage, and what we bequeath to future generations.

The research question was well framed and significant and the research was related to the existing body of knowledge in that it extended the present body of knowledge by expanding that body of knowledge with an original contribution. The theoretical framework for the study was adequate and appropriate and the researchers communicated clearly and fully. The research method was appropriate and the researchers effectively used a number of tables, graphs, charts, and streams of mathematical adjustments to the data sets to describe their research. There may be a better way to find answers to the research questions, but it would have to be a radical departure from the systematic presentation given by the researchers. The sample size was sufficient and there were adequate controls for researcher bias.

The research should be replicable, using the same data sets and methodologies, and the limitations of the study were that the researchers concentrated on the actual energy emissions in order to find their results, versus actual energy usage. The results of the study should be generalizable, if we take into account the previous studies that used emissions for the theoretical groundwork and data sets studied. In this manner, the conclusions would be justified by the results.

Gligor, M., & Ausloos, M. (2007). Cluster structure of eu-15 countries derived from the correlation matrix analysis of macroeconomic index fluctuations. *The European Physical Journal, 57*(2), 139-146. DOI:

10.1140/epjb/e2007-00132-5, 2008, from Academic Search Premier.

Gligor and Ausloos (2007) utilized about one-dozen indices that were pertinent to the use of a macroeconomic model, to examine the flux of those data with regard to the correlation of the data from over one-dozen European countries. This was a study conducted of related frameworks with regard to data fluctuations in general. Two different methods were used and compared in the study that resulted in some conclusions about the applications of time series and the resulting correlations among those indices extant in the European countries' data. This study was important in that it compared two methods of analysis, in a different way from the study literature surveyed, and then applied them to a framework that could be used in an alternate way to model data and observe fluctuations among the macroeconomic indicators to reach some conclusions (p. 139). This made the article valuable in that it contributed to a better understanding of the field of macroeconomic modeling and some of the procedures that were useful for forecasting and prediction.

The research was framed and significant in that the clusters of data were examined by a comparison of the theoretical versus the methodological perspectives. The research related well to the existing body of knowledge and made an original contribution to that body of knowledge by extending the basis of present research surveyed in the article. The theoretical framework for the study was adequate and appropriate and the researchers communicated clearly and fully. The research method was appropriate and compared existing data sets, and the accompanying results, with the data sets and results from the study. There may be a better way to find answers to the research questions, but it would necessarily involve a sample size beyond the sufficient sample size utilized in this study. There were adequate controls for researcher bias and the research should be replicable, if the same methods were employed using the same data sets.

The limitations of the study were the 15 European countries, and the findings should be generalizable to this region as a baseline for further discussions. If the region examined were used to draw some further conclusions with regard to the specific region examined as a result of this study, the conclusions should be justified by the results.

Gottschalk, R. (2005). The macro content of prsps: Assessing the need for a more flexible macroeconomic policy framework. *Development Policy Review, 23*(4), 419-442. DOI: 10.1111/j.1467-7679.2005.00295.x, 2008, from Academic Search Premier database.

Gottschalk (2005) surveyed 15 trade studies conducted on the operation of the conduct of the reduction of poverty. The researcher claimed that those studies, in the "developed" countries involved in those surveyed studies, did not allow for the requisite malleability that would be necessary to compensate for shocks from outside the macroeconomic systems examined. Further, those models failed to appropriately consider the nature of the inherent "volatility" that would be secondary to the outside shocks peculiar to those systems. The researcher claimed that the domestic policies in the countries surveyed were so provincial, and were so centered upon an equilibrium mindset, that the outside shocks adversely affected "poverty and growth." The researcher suggested a more loosely configured set of controls that would eventually lead to more attainable target levels for pricing and inflation in the economies examined. Further, the researcher concluded that there would be more allowances built in to the proposed systems to compensate for the prevalent external shocks and that those measures would provide for "the adoption of permanent safety nets." This study was important in that it addressed an alternate solution to apparent shortfalls in the types of conventional thinking that had already been published in a number of previous studies (p. 419). The article was valuable in that it considered an alternate solution to those shortfalls, and demonstrated a viable framework for the pursuit of that solution, with regard to the forecasting and prediction associated with macroeconomic solutions, through the use of computational modeling.

The research question was well framed and significant, and the research related well to the existing body of knowledge by extending it in an alternate direction. The research made an original contribution to the existing body of knowledge by indicating where the current research had ignored some pertinent factors, concerning models, and it demonstrated a meaningful way of solving those issues. The theoretical framework for the study was adequate and appropriate and the researcher communicated clearly and fully. The research methods were appropriate. There may be a better way of finding the answers to the research questions, but it would necessarily involve a much larger sample size than the adequate sample size used in this study. There were adequate controls used to compensate for researcher bias.

The study research should be replicable, if the same data sets and the same statistical methods were used. The limitations of this study were that middle-income countries were used for the data sets in the model, so the findings of the study would certainly be generalizable to those sorts of countries. If the findings were used in this manner, then the conclusions were justified by the results.

Gyurkovics, E., Meyer, D., & Takacs, T. (2007). Budget balancing in a two-dimensional macroeconomic model. *Mathematical and Computer Modelling of Dynamical Systems, 13*(2), 179-192. DOI: 10.1080/13873950600739034, 2008, from Academic Search Premier database.

Gyurkovics, Meyer, and Takacs (2007) conducted a study that used two theoretical players in a strategic game that modeled a private economic player against the government. The government, as one might expect, utilized various fiscal policies and the private player was guaranteed "cost control." Unfortunately, there was a nebulous consideration for labor, because the rate of economic improvement was unknown for this factor. So in conventional terms, with regard to Nash Equilibria and similar sorts of strategic games, it would have been just about impossible to obtain "an optimal solution." The purpose of the strategic game was to demonstrate, since the private player was guaranteed cost control in the face of the worst possible circumstances where the government player showed extremely high debt balances, that "balancing" was still possible as an end-product to the strategic game even when "the volume of fixed capital stock is lower than the equilibrium value." The study was important because it was allowed, through a strategic game macroeconomic model simulation, to model the worst case scenario and still derive, in the face of stringent assumptions, a workable solution to a modern issue that has plagued some economies, at different times, all over the world (p. 179). The article was valuable in that it provided a prospective solution, within the narrow confines of the study's assumptions, to solve a problem that occurs in economies from time to time.

The research question was well framed and significant in that it related well to the existing body of knowledge and extended that body of knowledge with an innovative solution to a problem that repeatedly occurred in the studies surveyed. As a result of the innovative solution provided, it made an original contribution to the existing body of knowledge. The theoretical framework for the study was adequate and appropriate and the researchers communicated clearly and fully. The research method was appropriate, but made some considerably restrictive assumptions to make the methodology functional. The monotonic nature of the computational modeling performed *in vitro*, might make the actual usefulness of the model *in vivo* questionable because of the number of restrictive assumptions originally used to make the model functional. The sample size was sufficient. There may be a better way to find the answers to the research questions, but it would have to be done in a different manner with other assumptions, which would have considerably changed the entire study and made some of the macroeconomic model's restrictive assumptions problematic.

There were adequate controls for researchers' bias and the research should be replicable with the same data sets and procedures that were utilized in the original study. The limitations of the study were the restrictive assumptions utilized to make the macroeconomic computational model functional. Therefore, the generalizability of the study could be limited to the theoretical aspect of the conclusions and the study's findings, unless a perfect scenario that duplicated the model's results actually occurred in the real world. Therefore, if we keep the assumptions and restrictions of the conclusions in this aforementioned perspective, the conclusions would be justified by the results.

Holden, S., & Wulfsberg, F. (2007). How strong is the macroeconomic case for downward real wage rigidity? *Research Review, 7*, 22-24. Accession Number 26614456, 2008, from Academic Search Premier database. Working paper of the Federal Reserve Bank of Boston, W-07-6. Full text downloaded from http://www.bos.frb.org/economic/wp/wp2007/wp0706.pdf.

Holden and Wulfsberg (2007) examined the macroeconomic aspects of "downward real wage rigidity (DRWR)" with the use of computational macroeconomic models to forecast the comparisons between real wage rigidity and nominal wage rigidity. The statistical approaches that the researchers used took into account variations in the data, with regard to the eccentricities of nationally or annually exclusive data sets, and examined the averages and distributions of wage data, taking into account environmental factors such as inflation and other variables. The researchers examined data from about 20 countries in and around North America, Scandinavia, and Europe. Economically, a researcher's intuition might lead to the thought that real wage rigidity, or wages adjusted for the prevalence and strength of contemporary inflation, would be more rigid. However, the researchers found that there were strong statistical indications that lead to the conclusion that there was "stronger evidence for downward nominal wage rigidity than for downward real wage rigidity." The article was important to contemporary research in that it found a difference in perceived downward wage rigidity that was contrary to the trade articles surveyed (p. 1). The article was valuable in that it demonstrated an alternate view to contemporary scholarly opinion concerning DRWR. The researchers were able to demonstrate that there was a lower incidence of diluted wages, adjusted for inflation, in nations that protected employees with union activity and government policies that protected those workers.

The research question was well framed and significant in that it related well to the existing body of knowledge and extended that body of knowledge with an innovative solution to a problem that repeatedly occurred in the studies surveyed. As a result of the innovative solution provided, the study made an original contribution to the existing body of knowledge. The theoretical framework for the study was adequate and appropriate and the researchers communicated clearly and fully. The research method was appropriate, but made some considerably restrictive assumptions to make the methodology functional. The sample size was sufficient. There may be a better way to find the answers to the research questions, but it would have to be done in a different manner with other assumptions, which would have considerably changed the entire study and made most of the macroeconomic model's restrictive assumptions untenable.

There were adequate controls for researchers' bias and the research should be replicable with the same data sets and procedures that were utilized in the original study. The limitations of the study were the restrictive assumptions utilized to make the macroeconomic computational model functional. Therefore, the generalizability of the study could be limited to the data aspect restrictions of the conclusions and the study's findings as they related to the 19 countries of data sets utilized to perform this study. Therefore, if we keep the assumptions and restrictions of the conclusions within this previously mentioned perspective, the conclusions would be justified by the results.

Ireland, P., & Schuh, S. (2006). Productivity and U.S. macroeconomic performance: Interpreting the past and predicting the future with a two-sector real business cycle model. *Research Review, 5*, 22-24. Accession Number 23674768, 2008, from Academic Search Premier database. Working paper of the Federal Reserve Bank of Boston, No. W-06-10. Full text downloaded from http://www.bos.frb.org/economic/wp/wp2006/wp0610.pdf.

Ireland and Schuh (2006) contrasted the internal U.S. economy, through the use of a macroeconomic forecasting model that depicted the multiple sectors of capital goods and consumption, as they related to allocated factors, and statistically found that there was a pronounced difference between the sluggishness of the 1970's and the boom economy, related to "investment-specific" growth, of the 1990's. The researchers predicted that the boom economy of the 1990's would not occur again with any predictable frequency, and that the post-war sluggish economy of the 1970's was attributable to decreased levels of consumption goods. The importance of this article was that it forecasted the recession of the early 21st century, in the U.S. economy, in oblique terms (p. 1). The value of this article was that it extended the literature survey by demonstrating that this two-sector, computational, macroeconomic model was workable, manageable, and was significant with regard to forecasting and economic prediction.

The research question was well framed and significant in that it related well to the existing body of knowledge and extended that body of knowledge with an insight into a problem that was addressed in the studies surveyed. As a result of the conclusions found, it made an original contribution to the existing body of knowledge. The theoretical framework for the study was adequate and appropriate and the researchers communicated clearly and fully. The research method was appropriate. The sample size was sufficient. There may be a better way to find the answers to the research questions, but it would have to be done in a different manner with other assumptions, which would have considerably changed the entire study and made some of the macroeconomic model's restrictive assumptions useless.

There were adequate controls for researchers' bias and the research should be replicable with the same data sets and procedures that were utilized in the original study. The limitations of the study were the restrictive annual data sets utilized to make the macroeconomic computational model functional. Therefore, the generalizability of the study could be limited to the aspect of the data set specific conclusions and the study's findings. Therefore, if we keep the assumptions and restrictions of the conclusions in this previous perspective, the conclusions would be justified by the results.

Jeske, K. (2005). Macroeconomic models with heterogeneous agents and housing. *Economic Review, 90*(4), 39-56. Accession Number 19489004, 2008, from Academic Search Premier database.

Jeske (2005) surveyed several dozen trade articles, in his current research survey, that all addressed the topical tenets of macroeconomic modeling with regard to related agents that tie the factors concerning the housing market in the U.S. to the U.S. economy. The researcher indicated that this was significant research because the housing market was practically double the size of the U.S.'s annual GDP and the movement of this much capital had a profound effect on the entire economy. The researcher tied four articles in to his research in order to reach the conclusion that housing and the policies of the government profoundly affect the finance involved with household income and the economy in general. The researcher realized that age, income, and net worth all played critical roles, in addition to household diversity, with regard to the finance portfolios of real estate and government's roles in the economy. The article was important to the field of macroeconomic modeling because it demonstrated the power of this computational sort of forecasting and economic prediction, with relation to the ability to develop trending, to assist with fiscal policy management for the government.

The research question in this study was well framed and significant in that it related well to the existing body of knowledge and extended that body of knowledge. As a result of the conclusions found, it made an original contribution to the existing body of knowledge. The theoretical framework for the study was adequate and appropriate and the researchers communicated clearly and fully. The research method was appropriate. The sample size was sufficient. There may be a better way to find the answers to the research questions, but it would have to be done with an alternate type of macroeconomic model, which would have considerably changed the entire study and made some of the macroeconomic model's restrictive assumptions useless.

There were adequate controls for researchers' bias and the research should be replicable with the same data sets and procedures that were utilized in the original study. The limitations of the study were that the data was principally re-used from the other four principal studies that were similar to this study and those data were taken from the survey. Therefore, the generalizability of the study could be limited to the aspect of the data set specific conclusions and the study's findings. Therefore, if we keep the assumptions and restrictions of the conclusions in this previous perspective, the conclusions would be justified by the results.

Kraev, E., & Akolgo, B. (2005). Assessing modelling approaches to the distributional effects of macroeconomic policy. *Development Policy Review, 23*(3), 299-312. DOI:10.1111/j.1467-7679.2005.00288.x, 2008, from Academic Search Premier database.

Kraev and Akolgo (2005) studied macroeconomic modeling and determined that there were four basic approaches to the types of models that could be used to formulate the foundations for fiscal policy determination: "*fixed ratio, econometric, CGE and microsimulation* models." After the researchers made that determination, they further concluded that there were five variables that could be modeled to optimize the formulations that would lead to adequate simulations that would result in effective fiscal policies. The researchers determined, of the four different models analyzed and studied, that the macroeconomic model that performed the most effectively consistently was the CGE model because, although it was afflicted with a number of anomalous shortcomings, the CGE model was the most effective all-around model for use with a variety of different types of data sets and parameters. This article was important to the field of macroeconomic modeling because it summarily dismissed several types of modeling approaches that do not perform well consistently with a variety of data sets and parameters (p. 299). The fact that it determined that the CGE model was best for most situations, could save a tremendous amount of time for the general researcher in computational macroeconomic modeling who might employ such results for fiscal policy formulations.

The research question in this study was well framed and significant in that it related well to the existing body of knowledge and extended that body of knowledge. As a result of the conclusions found, it made an original contribution to the existing body of knowledge. The theoretical framework for the study was adequate and appropriate and the researchers communicated clearly and fully. The research method was appropriate. The sample size was sufficient. There may be a better way to find the answers to the research questions, but it would have to be done with alternate types of macroeconomic models that would be different from the models utilized, which would have considerably changed the entire study and made some of the macroeconomic model's restrictive assumptions inapplicable to fiscal policy formulation.

There were adequate controls for researchers' bias and the research should be replicable with the same data sets and procedures that were utilized in the original study. The limitations of the study were that the data sets were principally re-used from the other studies that were similar to this study and those data were taken from the survey. The data was taken and re-used by each particular model type from the surveyed studies. Therefore, the generalizability of the study could be limited to the aspect of the data set specific conclusions drawn from the previous studies and this particular study's findings. Therefore, if we keep the assumptions and restrictions of the conclusions in this previous perspective, the conclusions would be justified by the results.

Makasheva, N. (2006). Once again about the revolution of J.M. Keynes (An attempt to construct a macroeconomic theory for an uncertain economy), *Social Sciences, 37*(4), 16-29. Accession Number 23293723, 2008, from Academic Search Premier database.

Makasheva (2006) basically performed an economic

history review of the economists from Adam Smith, through Keynes, up through Schumpeter, Samuelson, and Friedman. Although this was particularly entertaining to read, there seemed to be some uncertainty about the rationale for publishing what was mostly a review that could have been taken from just about any master's level graduate text on economic history. Although the text of the article, or "study," if it could loosely be addressed in that manner, was mildly interesting, it dismally attempted to address some theoretical tenets of possible or conceivable macroeconomic theory for computational modeling, but accomplished nothing. The theoretical segment accomplished very little theorizing and was basically composed of a review of past economic theory from an historic perspective. There was no data analysis, because no data were used in this study. Therefore, the dozen or so analysis questions to be fielded have been rendered moot.

Literature Review Essay

Introduction

This literature review essay builds upon the theoretical perspectives and critical analyses presented in the Breadth component of this paper by using those macroeconomic theorists, and the applicable parts of their respective theories, as a foundation for the discussion involving the current research that was introduced in the annotations above. The integrated focus of the annotated research articles discussed above is macroeconomic theory applied to Economic forecasting and computer simulations that are used by end consumers who formulate fiscal policy for aggregate economies. The outline of the organization of this literature survey includes major aspects of macroeconomic theory that is applied to Economic forecasting and computer simulation: size of the model; approaches to the modeling of macroeconomic policy; taxation; agent based macroeconomics; heterogeneous agents and effects on housing; space and time in a macroeconomic model; external aid on economic growth; macroeconomic consistency issues; matrix analysis of macroeconomic index fluctuations; effects of external shocks on fiscal and monetary policies; external shocks on production technologies; gaming and dimensions of macroeconomic models; forecasting with macroeconomic models; and simulations.

The rationale of the Depth narrative is to explore in detail these fourteen named aspects of Economic forecasting and computer simulation, as they relate to and bear upon macroeconomics and the theories espoused in the Breadth segment, to improve the reader's understanding of these subjects and provide a foundation for analyses, comparison, and contrast in the Application segment of this paper.

Size of the model

Campbell and Krane (2005) realized in their study that it would have been close to impossible to build a model that exactly duplicated the U.S. economy. Their first focus on the distributional impact of a macroeconomic model, that would be able to eventually guide policymakers with respect to fiscal policy, was to limit the size of the macroeconomic model's structure so that the model would be manageable. The chained mathematical equations simulated the simultaneous changes, of five different variables and placed certain restrictions on the theoretical aspects of the model, and the model was thus referred to as a stochastic model. The model designated income shocks and differentiated the temporary from the permanent anomalies to that income examined (p. 58). The named variables set, C, S, Y, B, and X, was described by the researchers; "consumption of nondurable goods and services, C_t...stock of durable goods, S_t...Labor income in period t is Y_t...face value of the bonds at the beginning of period t is B_t...X_t ...household's purchases of durable goods" (p. 53).

Nicholas Jewczyn

Campbell and Krane (2005) constructed a "small macroeconomic forecasting model of real economic activity and inflation." The small number of variables utilized in the chained, mathematical equations of the macroeconomic model assumed that nondurables and services consumption, based upon the permanent income theory, could tell the forecasters much about economic predictions of the long-run. National economic expenditures on "durable goods and total private income" were inconsistent with household "spending on nondurable consumption." Mathematically concluded, as a result of the minor, theoretical assumptions listed above and the forecasts generated by the chained equations, the model identified that the variance in the prediction error, regarding consumption, resulting from long-term shocks to income. Transient factors, resulting from the forecast predictions, were able to reconcile the short and near-term errors resulting in the variance of those forecasts. However, the main result determined that the long-run shocks to the model accounted "for between one-fifth and one-third of the variation in these variables at the two-year forecast horizon." Compared with the surveyed literature, this was a dramatic accuracy improvement of the consistency and predictability of the forecast horizon, and it concomitantly resulted in a smaller prediction error, improving the model's use for prediction and formulation of government fiscal policies (p. 67).

Approaches to the modeling of macroeconomic policy

Kraev and Akolgo (2005) examined various approaches regarding the modeling of macroeconomic policy. They reasoned, in their study, that there were five different group variable aspects with which a researcher should be concerned: "being able to represent policy levels used in the policy packages, allowing for both price- and quantity-clearing markets, integrating financial stocks, representing short-term dynamics, and providing measures of confidence in a model's output" (p. 299). The researchers knew that it was imperative to simulate the actual level of the variables that fell under government control in order to make the model accurate. So even though the money supply was important, it was important not to use it as an aggregate variable since money supply was determined by the central bank and not by the government. Thus, to be more accurate with respect to eventual forecasting and prediction, separate variables were used for monetary as well as fiscal policy prediction. This seemed to be a rational conclusion on the part of the researchers in order to segregate "non-monetary government liabilities and a fractional reserve banking system" (p. 300).

Kraev and Akolgo (2005) determined that in order to work with the second group of variables, the price and quantity clearing markets, it was important to not assume full-employment since untenable variations would occur in the model if one unemployed group had to be assumed to be automatically employed elsewhere doing something else. Thus, a breakdown of the second group of variables was partitioned to be: "variable employment and capacity utilisation [sic]; either quantity or relative price to be the dominant mode of adjustment in any given sector; both output and price impacts of aggregate demand; and an independent investment function." In this manner, the grouping was sub-divided into four separate variables so that a movement in one variable would not adversely affect the movement of the entire grouping (p. 301).

Kraev and Akolgo (2005) were able to integrate the third grouping, of financial stocks within the model, by sub-dividing this third group into a variety of variables. The researchers felt that it was important and "not advisable to separate the interactions between nominal and real variables into an aggregate macro model to be run separately from a real-side model representing sectoral structure" (p. 302). This rationale was employed by the researchers for three reasons. The first reason had to do with the accurate depiction of portfolio reallocation and nominal flows of financial stocks. Since certain occurrences, such as "capital flight," occurred due to portfolio redistribution, this was one consideration of the first reason. The second consideration of the first reason was the lack of the assumption of the state of equilibrium so that "the changes in stocks resulting from flow imbalances that feed back into the determination of flows" could automatically adjust the model. The second reason of the three, was that although the fractional reserve policies associated with central banking assumed money creation, there wasn't a guarantee that the maximum amount of money created thresh-hold would be reached (p. 302).

Kraev and Akolgo (2005) realized that since the secondary reserve ratio may be out of the limits of the economy and the model, "an adequate model of monetary policy should include both the central bank and the commercial banks as independent agents." The third, and most critical reason, was the relationships "between aggregate price level, output, and the money supply, and the closely related issue of the causes of persistent inflation in many developing countries." The researchers realized that monetarism related the active supply of money to "demand-pull inflation" and the level of price moved between the amounts of central bank issued money and the cash needs of the private sector. Tight policies on credit could reduce inflation, but have just a negligible effect upon output. "Cost-push inflation" that came into effect, as described by the structuralist theorists, was secondary to conflicts arising from profit-taking by producers, who raised prices, and real-wage protectionism resulting from labor's attempts to raise nominal wages. Another consideration was the mandate for working capital and investment credit. Thus, for the third reason, the inherent model had to account for the "impact of monetary policy on output and inflation to allow for both alternatives to hold at different times, and to be able to switch between them, depending on the current state of the economy" (p. 303).

Kraev and Akolgo (2005) believed some interesting assumptions for the fourth grouping. The researchers maintained that, due to many changes in policy and external shocks to the economic system, that there was no such thing as equilibrium over the long-term, because "long-term equilibrium is never actually achieved." The researchers believed this rather remarkable assumption for two particular reasons. Since anomalies and shocks to a system were usually "nonlinear," this meant that the forecasting accuracy of a macroeconomic model, in developing economies, that relied upon "long-term equilibria is likely to be low." The second support for their assumption was that the dynamics associated with short-term forecasting was just as important in the designing of certain policy as long-term results from economic shocks (p. 303).

Kraev and Akolgo (2005) realized, for the fifth grouping that provides measures of confidence in a model's output, that researchers who model macroeconomic policy can place a number of disclaimers on the output from models, since the forecasted results are not always consistent or accurate. This study's researchers felt that if the numbers were not accurate, that they would not be able to draw inferences from the model to provide an accurate forecast at all. So the researchers felt that there were three important virtues that a model should possess, with regard to output generated:

(i)   the degree to which the model's output is determined by its assumptions as opposed to the data used in calibration;
(ii)   the degree to which the model is able to reproduce historical data; and
(iii) the range of parameter values and predictions that a model can produce while still reproducing the values used in its calibration. (p. 304)

Their important realization of the fact that these virtues were extremely difficult to obtain in the output from a macroeconomic model, did not minimize their importance with regard to the eventual macroeconomic forecast used to determine fiscal policy.

Taxation

Garner (2005) pursued the Bush Administration's mandate for tax reform with the suggestion to move the U.S.'s federal tax from an income based tax to a consumption based tax. The rationale for this leap in logic was that economists in this literature survey surmised that "switching to a consumption tax could increase saving and real output per person over the long run" (p. 5). The results of that survey showed that the consensus felt that, in the long-run however, there was disagreement about effect size. For the short-run, the consensus felt that there would be turmoil on the part of monetary policy formulation and that there would be considerable adjustments necessary to the economy (p. 5).

Garner (2005) mandated that there were five main goals associated with tax reform, with regard to fiscal policy formulation: "simplicity, stability, fairness, adequate revenue, and economic efficiency" (p. 6). Garner further noted that there were three basic types of consumption taxes, as viable alternatives to the federal income tax wherein almost half of the federal tax receipts were appropriated through a federal personal income tax:

"a national retail sales tax, a value-added tax (VAT), and a flat tax" (p. 11).

Garner (2005) determined that, of the three types of consumption tax as a substitute or replacement for the federal income tax, that the most viable consumption tax was the flat tax. The researcher found evidence that the use of either a value-added tax or a sales tax indicated that there would be potential issues with prices and wages and that this usage would require a larger transitional, economic adjustment. The researcher sided with economists from the literature survey in that "switching from an income tax to a consumption tax will lower the pretax interest rate" (p. 21). The real key, determined in the study, was to have the legislative bodies move to quickly enact some exact protocols, so that the Federal Reserve could make some decisions about monetary policy with regard to levels of consumer pricing. So, how the monetary policy was set after the legislative instructions were promulgated to the Federal Reserve, would determine "whether a consumption tax would lead to an increase in prices or a decrease in wages...either approach would involve difficult decisions affecting nominal price or wage contracts and the real value of existing assets" (p. 22). Since the federal income tax was depicted as convoluted and confusing by the researcher, the consumption tax may prove to be the best alternative, if it is properly enacted, monitored and adjusted for minimal economic impact in the short-run indicators, with the long-run impacts for price and wage adjustment that grow the economy.

Agent based macroeconomics

Chen (2005) addressed research trending in over fifty papers in the literature survey of this study. Chen described the advent of two considerations with regard to agent-based macroeconomic forecasting and computational modeling: "first, the extensive applications of computational intelligence tools in modeling adaptive behavior, and second the grounding of these applications in the cognitive sciences" (p. 3). This study was a follow-up to a previous study, and the two points addressed in this study were precluded from the original study.

There were two critical points involved with the first consideration of computational tools with regard to Chen's (2005) modeling adaptive behavior: the extension of rather straight-forward behavior to more involved behavior that is adaptive and the second has to do with the "*behavioral foundations* of agent engineering" (p. 5). One of the basic suppositions of macroeconomic "agent-based modeling" is the engineering aspects with regard to agents in particular. The actual agents' behavior was enriched through the use of significant use of the economics derived from computational intelligence. Since the variables were basically depicted as a series of numbers in data sets, the parametric equations were rather elementary. However, when the use of "rules" was integrated into the computational models, there was more interpretation and adjustment to those models and the behavior became more complex and thus more realistic (p. 4).

The second part of the computational intelligence development was the basic framework of the CI computations. Since the general computer algorithms were not very adaptable to the theoretical constructs, the previous advent of the rules lead to the use of "*interviews* and *questionnaires*" that were then used in overseas markets to predict exchanges and rates. The laboratory data that resulted from the use of humans in sociology research was applied as "*reinforcement learning*" and further demonstrated that "agent-based economic models *can* benefit from *experimental economics*" (p. 5).

The second consideration had to do with the way that humans process information or quite simply - cognition. The study suggested that the human "ability to process information efficiently is the outcome of *Applying fuzzy logic* as part of our thought process. Evidence on human reasoning and human thought processes supports the hypothesis that at least some categories of human thought are definitely fuzzy" (p. 5). Early agent behavior studies decided that the behavior that would adapt was more distinct. But the recent study concluded that part of human behavior was "fuzzy." There has been no suggestion to date that Wall Street traders were fuzzy or simple in thought, however, and the application of the fuzzy thinking system, or "the *genetic-fuzzy classifier system* (GFCS) to model traders' adaptive behavior in an artificial stock market," has alleviated the human mind's predisposition to confuse more complex issues. Evidence suggested that the conventional human mind "is notoriously bad at intuitively comprehending exponential growth." So, the importance of the GFCS system that was used to model trader behavior was that it provided more accurate results due to the fact that the reasoning load on human agents was decreased. According to the study, this provided more accurate results and it promoted accuracy of the model for real-world uses. The results of the study suggested that "agent-based modeling should have closer interactions with *the field and panel study, experimental economics* and *behavioral economics"* (pp. 5-6).

Heterogeneous agents and effects on housing

Jeske (2005) surveyed studies that indicated that the U.S. housing sector amounted to 1 1/2 times the U.S. Annual

Gross Domestic Product and that the real estate in the household portfolios amounted to a significant portion of the wealth retained by U.S. households in general. The impact of uniform agents in the economy, as a result of the retained wealth in those real estate portfolios, became significant determinants of economic activity and the researcher sought to study the activities of those uniform agents and how they determined the macroeconomic movements in the U.S. economy. The survey determined that, with regard to household debt, real estate loans (the mortgage market was found to be slightly less than half the size of the real estate market) were in aggregate four times larger than the sum total of credit card and automobile debt combined, for U.S. households. The survey showed the researcher that "Net worth, housing value (gross and net of mortgages), and income vary substantially among households not only by age but within age groups." The macroeconomic research depicted in the survey went to considerable lengths to employ these factors as input into the models of economic activity in the U.S. Although heterogeneous agents were used in the researcher's models, those heterogeneous agents were broken down into the quoted sub-categories to provide a more realistic contribution, from the housing market, into the model simulation in this study. There was considerable diversity noted among the breakdowns of the heterogeneous agents in the housing market to account for this variable segregation in the model (p. 39).

Jeske (2005) employed in this study the conventional belief that it was necessary to utilize heterogeneous agents in the model, with respect to housing in general, because "An economic model with heterogeneous agents is therefore necessary to measure the effects a price increase might have on agents with different incomes and asset holdings" (p. 40). The primary reason for this type of necessity, holding the basis of heterogeneity as a constant, was to determine which type of mortgage was best suited to the more youthful population in the study so that the appropriate instrument could be chosen for their special needs. The youthful population, it was found, had more issues with the size and availability of the down payment and the type of mortgage needed to reflect this to make housing more accessible. The youthful market participants were more likely to compete and were able to compete successfully when mortgages were subsidized. This did not necessarily give the youthful mortgage holders more of an advantage, but leveled the playing field so that that they had access in general, not better access to funds to make home ownership a reality. The study, holding heterogeneity as a constant, determined that the subsidy made housing more affordable and brought more wealth into the economy in general. Thus, the housing market was not reserved for the wealthy or the elderly - the youthful participants were able to participate on a larger scale because of the mortgage subsidies. The fiscal policy implications from the results of the study mentioned that the ingress of the youthful participants changed the macroeconomic policy implications and that these results needed to be accounted for in the fiscal policy formulations predicted by the study's simulation results (p. 40).

Space and time in a macroeconomic model

Foote (2007) surveyed a number of studies and chose one to update. He took a study by Shimer and updated it by extending the time period of the data set and by altering the nature of the data set. Foote found that the data in the regional panel were unreliable and he actually changed the results of the previous study by expanding the data set's time frame sample period and by extending the amount of data beyond the regional panel data sets used in the original study. By using state level data, he determined that the accuracy of the previous data was in question and that the original results changed because of the changes in the study updates. Foote realized that there was now a positive correlation between the effect of youth and the unemployment figures and this result more closely resembled what a traditional model would produce for expected results. Even with the large errors secondary to the model, the study showed that there was indeed a positive correlation between the age of the prospective employee and unemployment in general.

External aid on economic growth

Genberg (2005) surveyed current research that discussed the impact of outside financial aid upon economic growth in developing countries. He realized that in order to accurately model the relationship between foreign aid and an economy's economic growth, that it was necessary that "empirical work must be based more explicitly on structural models of the link between aid and growth, notably by incorporating relationships between aid, government fiscal responses, private sector investment, and economic growth" (p. 1). He realized in the end that even though the external aid financial programs could have had an effective design, that the manifestation of those aid programs in the domestic economy was eventually a function of the effectiveness of the use of those programs and how much funding was provided by the receiving nation to match those foreign funds and implement them for economic growth. Regardless of how well the foreign aid program was designed, the effectiveness of the program also had a great deal to do with how stable the receiving country's political and social climate was and how those two considerations affected the manifestation and use of the aid received for actual programs in the receiving country. Also, if the aid was the result of the principle of conditionality, then the manifestation of the aid and required funds to match that aid could be skewed and could profoundly affect the proposed or planned economic growth the could have or even should have resulted in the receiving country's economy. More study on the long-term effects of such constraints and the accompanying model's parameters is needed (p. 37).

Macroeconomic consistency issues

Ghersi and Hourcade (2006) realized the ideological inconsistency, from their literature survey, of the top-down versus the bottom-up inter-relationships between the "energy-economy-environment (E3) linkages" that the literature had attempted to combine. They attempted to consider the vast array of high-tech data available for the energy forecasts from resources input and the eventual "macroeconomic implications of public policies," but they discovered a larger issue in their survey. There was a basic lack of consistency between change in the technology of the economy and the change associated with only the energy sector's technology. Their study attempted to resolve this consistency issue by isolating only the traditional gap "between the engineer's and the economist's descriptions of energy technologies" (p. 39).

Ghersi and Hourcade (2006) were able to segregate their research in this study into just three sub-categories. The researchers put together a framework that addressed only "endogenous technical change." The second research point was a particular study methodology that addressed non-dynamic functions and production and the third was to addresses the fluctuations, caused by policy, away from the previously accepted energy projections. All three of these categories were directly related to the "Cobb-Douglas function" that depicted all of the two dozen different types of energy service to households, instead of aggregate macroeconomic production of the United States' economy, and the segregation became elementary: subtract everything from the equation except for the energy produced in order to model just that. There were some constancy issues associated with the model's constraints, but the macroeconomic model was an engine that worked well to produce forecasts and solve the consistency issues, with macroeconomic data, that the researchers had found in their literature survey (p. 40).

Matrix analysis of
macroeconomic index fluctuations

Gligor and Ausloos (2007) gave a very detailed description in their study of variables used in their simulation model that addressed country distances, windows with regard to time averages, and tree spanning models, but in reality, the study was a fancy version of a linear programming transportation model (used in M.B.A. programs to depict *least cost moves* of physical stock from a few warehouse locations to many manufacturing plants that take the raw materials and partially completed stock to produce finished piece goods). Once the reader realized this fact, the rest of the manipulations and sophisticated terms were just window dressing. The main focus of the way in which the computer algorithm was devised in this study, was that it "decoupled" or basically removed the macroeconomic index fluctuations from the core of the model and addressed them separately. The researchers used about one dozen indicators to determine that European Union countries demonstrated regionally biased statistics because the macroeconomic values of those countries regionally moved in "clusters" (p. 139).

Gligor and Ausloos (2007) used some principles from their literature survey in this study. They continued the train of thought that the field of Physics could contribute to the time series analysis of macroeconomic indicators with the use of "random matrix theory (RMT), initially developed in nuclear physics, also successfully used in the study of canonical correlations between stock changes and [a] portfolio optimization problem" (p. 140). This avenue of study, combined with "nonequilibrium networks" allowed the researchers to formulate a computer simulation that utilized the 11 variables to produce the cluster results necessary to prove the macroeconomic indicator fluctuation biases that they advanced in this study. To summarize the entire article in one sentence, the researchers determined that these clusters of regional data basically indicated that the European Union countries, by region, were biased against the trade of non-member nations. There were minor points described in the article that published the study, but the main point in the conclusions was the trade bias against non-member nations (p. 140).

Effects of external shocks on fiscal and monetary policies

Gottschalk (2005) analyzed the current literature concerning published studies, which worked to reduce poverty, and found that the current literature depicted regimes that were inflexible concerning policy formulation. The country studies surveyed failed to account for enough flexibility, regarding shocks that were outside the system, which affected the macroeconomic, aggregate economy of those nations. The researcher determined that the studies explained systems that were rigid and too provincial concerning the economic unrest in the systems examined and the frameworks only took into account, through various types of monetary and fiscal remediation, the budgetary balances and pricing schedules without allowing for the input and residual effects of external shocks and the inherent volatility engendered by the economic systems examined. The real value of this study came from the results portion that suggested a remedial approach that would allow for a less strict set of goals for inflation and fiscal management. In this way, the basic input pricing and stop-gap measures for fiscal policy adjustment could be placed in line with business cycle fluctuations in the economies examined (p. 419).

Gottschalk (2005) proposed a more international mindset for the determination of domestic macroeconomic policy. He realized that external shocks to the economy, which stemmed from international trade contracts that were too restrictive and weather phenomena that caused devastation to the countries examined, caused distress to the lower income citizens of these low income countries.

Thus, the more relaxed framework of economic goals would allow smoothing of the data and eventually the results of the macroeconomic model simulations and would provide better input for fiscal and monetary policy formulation (p. 420). The reason for this stemmed from the rationale that the researcher found that "external shocks and macroeconomic volatility on the premise that volatility is bad for both growth and poverty reduction" (p. 421).

External shocks on production technologies

Ireland and Schuh (2006) utilized a cyclical model in their study that represented real fluctuations in the modeled, hypothetical economy that only contained two sectors. The variables used were comprised of realistic external shocks to the modeled economy concerning productivity of goods that served investment and domestic consumption so that the input productivity could be varied with modeled growth or the lack of it. Part of the study's results claimed that the 1970's economic slowdown was a direct result of the lack of productivity stemming from lower levels of goods for consumption produced and that the eventual result was a reduction in goods for investment. The eventual productivity increase in the 1990's was just a means for the business cycle to make back lost time and productivity and that the economic increase was to be short-lived. Due to the unique set of circumstances attributable to the economic boom discussed, since it was apparently anomalous, the rationale was put forth that such an economic upsurge would not recur for quite some time (p. 1).

Ireland and Schuh (2006) applied their model simulation to a data set that contained data accumulated after the Second World War. The U.S. data sets were used to model external shocks concerning rates of growth and adjustments to production activities in the two sector model that concerned production of investment and consumption goods. The external technological shocks to the system were directly applied to various contrived variables that represented labor hours, proposed investment, and total consumption. The researchers then proceeded to examine the model's hypothetical results and compared the results with the historical results to make some assumptions about technological shocks to the system and how those shocks affected the investment and consumption goods sectors. In this way, the researchers were able to look at the historical impact of those external technological shocks, examine the volatility from the model and the actual occurrences, and thus better predict future anomalous shocks to these sectors in order to prepare for the advent of the external shocks with fiscal policy formulation (p. 2).

Gaming and dimensions of macroeconomic models

Gyurkovics, Meyer, and Takacs (2007) modeled a simulation between two players in an economy. The government and the private sector were the two players in these simulations of "two-person zero-sum nonlinear difference games" that were constrained by uncertainty and the players were in conflict. Given the manner in which the study was constructed, there could be no optimized solution, as in a Nash Equilibrium strategic game, but the model resulted in a number of alternate solutions and the researchers were placed in the position of having to choose the least-worst solution given by the computer model for macroeconomic policy formulation. The difference game was constructed so that the government player must engage in cost control while the private sector player was allowed to indulge in investment and "private consumption." The composite macroeconomic model exhibited by player 2, or the private sector, was an aggregated group of players opposing the government during the conflict scenario in the game. Essentially, the game was fiscal policy versus private consumption in order to derive a marginal-optimal solution for the formulation of aggregate, macroeconomic fiscal policy. The researchers determined that everything, with regard to fiscal policy formulation when the private sector and the government failed to cooperate, was essentially a goal driven trade-off with no optimal solution (p. 180).

Forecasting with macroeconomic models

Campbell and Krane (2005) constructed a variety of models in their study to perform forecasting for the evolution of macroeconomic policy formulation. Part of the constraints in their model reflected low volatility and "stable inflation" from the time period of the 1980's because this implied better control issues for macroeconomic results and thus better implications for eventual fiscal policy formulation. The researchers maintained that the use of sample limits implied that they were by default restricted to a smaller number of parameters that could be used in the model's estimation of macroeconomic factors. Their literature review specified a number of economic theory objections to a larger number of parameters and thus implied that the limited parameters utilized in the model in the study were necessary. After application of macroeconomic theory from the literature review, they spent a considerable amount of effort describing the data and the application of those data to the empirical model. The researchers moved to explanations of results derived from the model's estimations and then discussed projected forecasts derived from the model's simulations. The primary reason behind this level of intimacy with the data and the model itself was to "discuss the use of our model to measure and forecast the gap between actual output and its long-run potential level" (p. 53). The key to this study was that the researchers were able to demonstrate that there was now a way, as a result of this study, to measure the difference between economic output and the long-run level forecasted. The implications for this are that rational agents could now adjust their consumption accordingly with prior knowledge and thus be able to impact consumption and investment in the aggregate economy changing the eventual price level in the long-run (p. 53).

Chen (2005) surveyed the previous studies that conducted forecasting with macroeconomic models and found that the researchers had used regression models that treated economic behavior in a linear sense, rather than through parametric adaptations of that behavior. Thus, the former research had made progress by introducing agents that moved about the economy by using formal rules of behavior, but the economic agents never engaged in adaptive economic behavior and none of the traditionally accepted adaptive or learned behavior was taken into account by these rudimentary economic models. The researcher realized that better models were created in the later studies surveyed that used parametric analyses and modeled this learned or adaptive behavior in a non-linear, parametric sense that evolved with the model to make more accurate economic forecasts based upon more realistic agent behaviors. The real starting point for the researcher's study came from literature that suggested that neither the linear nor the parametric approach would be effective to accurately model the economic behavior of agents in a theoretical economy. The researcher used models from the latest research based upon "genetic programming" that allowed the agents to "*think* and *reason*," which provided more realistic results in the economic model and allowed the researcher to make forecasts that were more in line with realistic situations depicting those agents in the theoretical economy of the model simulation. The agents were allowed, in the model, to demonstrate cognition abilities and thus were allowed to make strategic choices about their predicted behavior. This ultimately lead the researcher to be able to make more accurate predictions because the agents evolved with the model and the results produced more accurate forecasts for the resulting macroeconomic policy recommendations (p. 4).

Ireland and Schuh (2006) incorporated six particular

shocks into the simulation model to make forecasts. Since they were dealing with the production of investment goods and consumption goods, they produced three variables, rate of growth, levels and work-hours, for each of the two main groups. These six variables were then fed data by the model and the programming continued until the researchers realized some unprecedented findings: the investment results did not affect the consumption results. The consumption results were inter-related and the finding then had an impact upon the investment group variables. The severity of the consumption productivity shocks had larger effects upon each of the related consumption variables and then the severity of those shocks, based upon the interplay of the consumption variables, then produced larger results upon the productivity of the investment goods. These results were then used to more effectively forecast the results for the economy and, as a result, make better quality predictions for fiscal policy determination (p. 17).

Simulations

Chen's (2005) study cast aspersions on the capital asset pricing model. The researcher indicated that, since this particular model was originally predicated upon a "general equilibrium setting," that it was no longer optimal for fund managers when it came to the consideration of economic behavior. This entire thought process was based upon the "agent-based co-evolutionary context" and its relationship to decision making by the fund managers, as well as the investors. The results of this study indicated that when risk-averse investors made their presence known in the market, the fund managers who continued to use the former optimality of the CAPM did not continue to exist in the marketplace. Therefore, the evolving trading strategies were more attractive to the investors who persisted, and were characterized by risk aversion, and this evolution of a risk-averse strategy tended to deplete the supply of fund managers who would not evolve and who continued to trade with the antiquated CAPM model. This "formula-agent approach" dovetailed with extant economic theory by proving that the "economic behavior predicted by the economic theory is tested by directly adding formula agents to the initial population." This sort of simulation seemed to be self-perpetuating in that the addition of the new agents propagated the prediction of economic behavior that the study seemed to be trying to prove (p. 8).

The Dabla-Norris and Feltenstein (2005) study was predicated upon the revelation that "model simulations show that in the absence of budgetary flexibility to adjust expenditures, raising tax rates too high drives firms into the underground economy, thereby reducing the tax base"

(p. 153). This was hardly newsworthy, but the manner in which the researchers demonstrated this assertion, through the use of model simulations, was rather interesting. The most interesting thing in this study was that the researchers used internal and external variables, both of which have the tendency to make the results of the simulations applicable to policy formulations by a government. The manner in which the variables were constructed and applied allowed the results of the simulations, through interpretation, to be used with regard to the ferreting out of tax evaders who had proceeded to partake in the underground economies of the countries in question in this study. One means at the researchers' disposal was to run the model simulations forward in time in order to predict *how much* income should be derived from *how many* taxpayers. The exemplar in this first case was a projection of eight years forward in time. The key inter-relationship was between the real GDP and the nominal exchange rate. By demonstrating that there should be no stagnation at the conclusion of seven periods, the growth was indicative of the fact that businesses have partially enjoyed proceeds from the underground economy, or have fled the tax-base completely.

Garner (2005) realized and reported in this study that the principal result of a consumption tax was that new capital was perceived to be more valuable since the tax itself seemed to minimize the value of the pre-existing capital when compared with the introduction of the new capital. With this view in mind, the researcher maintained that the "proportional consumption tax" reduced the actual value of pre-existing capital by almost ten percent, which in turn was deleterious to the financial position of the elderly and the wealthy since they possessed much of the pre-existing capital. However, the researcher maintained that since the tax would occur only one time, that the tax itself would be beneficial in devaluing present assets by positively improving the effects of "real output." This effect was referred to as the "revenue-neutral consumption tax rate" and was supposed by the researcher to improve the lot of the economy in general because, since the elderly and wealthy households actually lost wealth, these households would then have to improve savings and increase work to compensate for any real losses to wealth in general (p. 19).

Garner (2005) observed, in the interpretation of the simulations resulting from the study's models, that the simulations depicted a variety of "trade-offs" looming in the distance that could confound fiscal reform goals. The biggest trade-off was the idea that economic progress gains, over the long-term, were traded for equitable application of the framework of tax reforms instituted. Since the tax code was already extremely complicated, any additional rules for the tax on consumption transition, or any sorts of deductions applied, would make the complexity of the already unwieldy code increase. The results of these simulations showed that policymakers who determined the fiscal rules, with regard to this sort of a proportional consumption tax, in conceiving of the reforms package or the stipulation of goal trade-offs, would have to make value judgments about the value of such a tax in general (p. 20).

Genberg's (2005) study focused upon adjustment lending, over a ten year period, and discussed the macroeconomic effects of that lending and how the lending promoted the growth of the economy by stimulating investment. The researcher's contention, from the results of the study and the use of simulation models, was that the growth was fostered indirectly in a non-linear manner. The old economic by-line that aid to countries to promote such economic growth was well received, when good macroeconomic policies were observed, was debunked because the aid fostered such growth indirectly and the good stewardship, intuitively assumed, that was necessarily implied was inapplicable (p. 2).

Genberg (2005) created structural models that simulated the "have" versus the "have-not" countries and determined that the results were predicated upon how those computer models were fed with independent and dependent data. The prediction validity was particularly associated with the approach and was "model-dependent." Since the results were strictly model-dependent, the appropriate linking between the variables and the economic policies proved to only be "as good as the models." The biggest detractor was some estimate of the fiscal policies that would have been extant without the introduction of such adjustment lending programs. So the crux of the research was predicated upon how credible the models were when those perceived or predicted policies that could have been in effect at the time of the prediction changed as result of the policy formulations suggested by the model simulations. In fact, the eventual results were what the reactions to those predictions were going to be in the economy at large (p. 27).

Ghersi and Hourcade (2006) concluded, with regard to the prediction potential for computer modeling and simulations in particular, that "the comparative-static analysis starts with ensuring that BU and TD no-policy projections portray the same world at the selected t+n horizon." In the world of energy production, projection with models has proven to be integral to the wise allocation of scarce economic resources. The previous statement assumes, or implies, that the value constructs in the simulations must be comparably applicable to the base-line for the overall energy sector at large. Without this particular model constraint, the simulation's results would be skewed. Another constraint to be observed, with relation to the adaptation of the model, was that the production and demand functions must be coordinated in order to make the results of the simulation relevant to the real world. The implication was that the entire range of energies that contain carbon, that would contribute to the overall future carbon footprint that we leave as a legacy to our progeny, should be broad enough in the function equations so that they would contain all of the "the asymptotic behavior of energy systems." The entire basis of this entire sequence of events, with relation to the constraints placed upon the simulations performed by computer, was that the range of the carbon energies were all determined by derivatives of partial pricing determined by the demand and production functions. The signaling of price was the primary determinant of the range specifications to make the models applicable to the real world, so the models were all price driven by partial derivatives (p. 44).

Gyurkovics, Meyer, and Takacs (2007) found that, with regard to computer model simulations, a balanced budget could depend upon the model's "uncertainty measure." This consideration, coupled with the modeling of the improvement of the quality of a proposed labor force, allowed the researchers to guarantee cost controls because there was no means of a guarantee in the model's simulation results without such improvement. Further considerations were the restraints built in to the model that included an adjustable volume of capital injected into the model and the unfavorable condition of "a huge amount of state debt" (p. 188).

Gyurkovics, Meyer, and Takacs (2007) assumed that the government, as a player in the simulation, had possession of virtually unlimited capital to inject into the model's simulation. There were some findings with regard to equilibrium values, with regard to the government, that suggested that a government could still balance a budget that was in arrears even when the "debt is higher and the volume of capital stock lower than the equilibrium value" (p. 190). The most important variable, however, was the determination of the quality input of labor. When the improvement of the labor force was taken into consideration, the simulation results moved in favor of the government away from the private sector player in the strategic gaming simulation (p. 190).

Holden and Wulfsberg (2007) performed their simulations on specific data sets instead of utilizing across the board averaging of variables in the data sets. In other words, the researchers assumed no wage rigidity for the study and derived "country-year" data notional statistical evaluations for the data shaping the curves based upon real versus the nominal wage growth data acquired during the study. The researchers accounted and adjusted for economic advancement, shocks, and other adverse sector phenomena that affect large data sets. They then compared projected wage reductions with actual wage reductions (notional versus empirical) and they found that if the notional cuts were proportionally larger than the actual wage cuts, then the trending was toward real downward wage rigidity. Most of the previous studies had been conducted upon nominal wage rigidity, so this study was considerably different from the literature surveyed. The researchers contended that nominal downward wage rigidity had been used as an indicator in past studies because "inflation serves as a vehicle for a coordinated reduction in real wages (as implied by Keynes' argument for the existence of downward nominal wage rigidity)." The researchers contended that the real wages were at issue (instead) and that agents in an ongoing economy should be interested in the downward real wage rigidity because of the interplay between wage rigidity and inflation. Since this affected agents' spending capital, the researchers found that this was more relevant to real world applicability and the prediction value associated with the simulation (p. 4).

Kraev and Akolgo (2005) determined from their

literature survey that there were a variety of issues that challenge the macroeconomist who models a computer simulation: "fiscal, monetary, exchange-rate, and trade measures presents [sic] a singularly interesting challenge" (p. 299). These considerations usually manifest as a group of challenges when considering the construction of a macroeconomic computer simulation to model the economy of a developing nation. The researchers found that it was important to consider macroeconomic goals or targets but that it was also important to consider the eventual results' policy implications with respect to manifestation effects within different sectors of the economy. These manifestations could affect the developing country's employment, income, poverty levels, output within the economy, and more. In order to solve these distributional issues, the researchers studied a variety of different simulation types and examined the associated methodologies. In working with the useful and ideal tenets of such modeling, the researchers narrowed the preferred types of simulation models down to four general types that were conventionally used in macroeconomic assessments of this nature. The researchers decided that there was one particular model that, although it did not always render exact results, was appropriate in most situations where this type of macroeconomic simulation was performed (p. 299).

Kraev and Akolgo (2005) decided that there were several constraints that should be written into a model simulation to make the results effective so that the prediction would be useful for macroeconomic policy formulation:

* variable employment and capacity utilisation [sic];
* either quantity or relative price to be the dominant mode of adjustment in any given sector;
* both output and price impacts of aggregate demand; and
* an independent investment function. (p. 301)

Kraev and Akolgo (2005) determined, after careful study of the four major types of simulation models, econometric, computable general equilibrium, microsimulation, and fixed ratio, that the computable (CGE) model was the most desirable, but not necessarily the most accurate producer of consistent results that were useful for macroeconomic policy formulation. There were two different types of CGE model that could be used, the most current use of which has been in the government market by traders who were interested in the non-monetary market sector such as bonds. The constraints of "full employment of labour [sic] and capital, sectoral adjustments driven by relative prices, and the aggregate price level being essentially driven by the money supply" characterize the CGE neoclassical model whereas the constraints of "quantity adjustments of output and cost-driven prices" characterize the structuralist CGE model type. The researchers were unclear about which of these two types of CGE models would be optimal. They did maintain that between the two types of the general CGE model types that most macroeconomic scenarios could be effectively modeled in developing countries. They determined that the continued use of the CGE model, versus the other three of the four total model types examined, would sacrifice some accuracy of prediction, and that the CGE model in general would consistently generate the highest quality result for fiscal policy formulation with macroeconomic modeling of developing country economies (p. 306).

Depth Summary

Campbell and Krane (2005) realized in their study that it would have been close to impossible to build a model that exactly duplicated the U.S. economy. Their first focus on the distributional impact of a macroeconomic model, that would be able to eventually guide policymakers with respect to fiscal policy formulation, was to limit the size of the macroeconomic model's structure so that the model would be manageable. Transient factors, resulting from the forecast predictions, were able to reconcile the short and near-term errors resulting in the variance of those forecasts. However, the main result determined that the long-run shocks to the model accounted for between one-fifth and one-third of the variation in these variables at the two-year forecast horizon. Compared with the surveyed literature, this was a dramatic accuracy improvement of the consistency and predictability of the forecast horizon, and it concomitantly resulted in a smaller prediction error, improving the model's use for prediction and formulation of government fiscal policies.

Kraev and Akolgo (2005) examined various approaches regarding the modeling of macroeconomic policy. They reasoned, in their study, that there were five different group variable aspects with which a researcher should be concerned: being able to represent policy levels used in the policy packages, allowing for both price- and quantity-clearing markets, integrating financial stocks, representing short-term dynamics, and providing measures of confidence in a model's output. This study's researchers felt that if the numbers were not accurate, that they would not be able to draw inferences from the model to provide an accurate forecast at all. So the researchers felt that there were three important virtues that a model should possess, with regard to output generated:

(i) the degree to which the model's output is determined by its assumptions as opposed to the data used in calibration;

(ii) the degree to which the model is able to reproduce historical data; and

(iii) the range of parameter values and predictions that a model can produce while still reproducing the values used in its calibration.

Their important realization of the fact that these virtues were extremely difficult to obtain in the output from a macroeconomic model, did not minimize their importance with regard to the eventual macroeconomic forecasts used to determine fiscal policy.

Garner (2005) pursued the Bush Administration's mandate for tax reform with the suggestion to move the U.S.'s federal tax from an income based tax to a consumption based tax. The rationale for this leap in logic was that economists in this literature survey surmised that switching to a consumption tax could increase saving and real output per person over the long run. The results of that survey showed that the consensus felt that, in the long-run however, there was disagreement about effect size. For the short-run, the consensus felt that there would be turmoil on the part of monetary policy formulation and that there would be considerable adjustments necessary to the economy.

Chen (2005) addressed research trending in over fifty papers in the literature survey of this study. Chen described the advent of two considerations with regard to agent-based macroeconomic forecasting and computational modeling: first, the extensive application of computational intelligence tools in modeling adaptive behavior, and second the grounding of these applications in the cognitive sciences. Evidence suggested that the conventional human mind was notoriously bad at intuitively comprehending exponential growth. So, the importance of the GFCS system that was used to model trader behavior was that it provided more accurate results due to the fact that the reasoning load on human agents was decreased. According to this study, this provided more accurate results and it promoted accuracy of the model for real-world uses. The results of the study suggested that agent-based modeling should have closer interactions with the field and panel study, experimental economics, and behavioral economics.

Jeske (2005) surveyed studies that indicated that the U.S. housing sector amounted to 1 1/2 times the U.S. Annual Gross Domestic Product and that the real estate in the household portfolios amounted to a significant portion of the wealth retained by U.S. households in general. The impact of uniform agents in the economy, as a result of the retained wealth in those real estate portfolios, became significant determinants of economic activity and the researcher sought to study the activities of those uniform agents and how they determined the macroeconomic movements in the U.S. economy. The survey determined that, with regard to household debt, real estate loans (the mortgage market was found to be slightly less than half the size of the real estate market) were in aggregate four times larger than the sum total of credit card and automobile debt combined, for U.S. households. The survey showed the researcher that net worth, housing value (gross and net of mortgages), and income vary substantially among households not only by age, but also within age groups.

Foote (2007) surveyed a number of studies and chose one to update. He took a study by Shimer and updated it by extending the time period of the data set and by altering the nature of the data set. Foote found that the data in the regional panel were unreliable and he actually changed the results of the previous study by expanding the data set's time frame sample period and by extending amount of data beyond the regional panel data sets used in the original study. By using state level data, he determined that the accuracy of the previous data was in question and that the original results changed because of the changes in the study updates. Foote realized that there was now a positive correlation between the effect of youth and the unemployment figures and that this result more closely resembled what a traditional model would produce for expected results.

Genberg (2005) surveyed current research that discussed the impact of outside financial aid upon economic growth in developing countries. He realized that in order to accurately model the relationship between foreign aid and an economy's economic growth, that it was necessary that the empirical work must be based more explicitly on structural models of the link between aid and growth, notably by incorporating relationships between aid, government fiscal responses, private sector investment, and economic growth. He realized in the end that even though the external aid financial programs could have had an effective design, that the manifestation of those aid programs in the domestic economy was eventually a function of the effectiveness of the use of those programs and how much funding was provided by the receiving nation to match those foreign funds and implement them for economic growth domestically.

Ghersi and Hourcade (2006) realized the ideological inconsistency, from their literature survey, of the top-down versus the bottom-up inter-relationships between the energy-economy-environment (E3) linkages that the literature had attempted to combine. They attempted to consider the vast array of high-tech data available for the energy forecasts from resources input and the eventual macroeconomic implications of public policies, but they discovered a larger issue in their survey. There was a basic lack of consistency between change in the technology of the economy and the change associated with only the energy sector's technology. Their study resolved this consistency issue by isolating only the traditional gap between the engineer's and the economist's descriptions of energy technologies.

Gligor and Ausloos (2007) gave a very detailed description in their study of variables used in their simulation model that addressed country distances, windows with regard to time averages, and tree spanning models, but in reality, the study was a fancy version of a linear programming transportation model (used in M.B.A. programs to depict least cost moves of physical stock from a few warehouse locations to many manufacturing plants that take the raw materials and partially completed stock to produce finished piece goods). Once the reader realized this fact, the rest of the manipulations and sophisticated terms were just window dressing. The main focus of the way in which the computer algorithm was devised in this study, was that it decoupled or basically removed the macroeconomic index fluctuations from the core of the model and addressed them separately. The researchers used about one dozen indicators to determine that European Union countries demonstrated regionally biased statistics because the macroeconomic values of those countries regionally moved in economic clusters.

Gottschalk (2005) analyzed the current literature concerning published studies, which worked to reduce poverty, and found that the current literature depicted regimes that were inflexible concerning policy formulation. The country studies surveyed failed to account for enough flexibility, regarding shocks that were outside the system, which affected the macroeconomic, aggregate economy of those nations. The researcher determined that the studies explained systems that were rigid and too provincial concerning the economic unrest in the systems examined and the frameworks only took into account, through various types of monetary and fiscal remediation, the budgetary balances and pricing schedules without allowing for the input and residual effects of external shocks and the inherent volatility engendered by the economic systems examined. The real value of this study came from the results portion that suggested a remedial approach that would allow for a less strict set of goals for inflation and fiscal management. In this way, the basic input pricing and stop-gap measures for fiscal policy adjustment could be placed in line with business cycle fluctuations in the economies examined.

Ireland and Schuh (2006) utilized a cyclical model

in their study that represented real fluctuations in the modeled, hypothetical economy that only contained two sectors. The variables used were comprised of realistic external shocks to the modeled economy concerning productivity of goods that served investment and domestic consumption so that the input productivity could be varied with modeled growth or the lack of it. Part of the study's results claimed that the 1970's economic slowdown was a direct result of the lack of productivity stemming from lower levels of goods for consumption produced and that the eventual result was a reduction in goods for investment. The eventual productivity increase in the 1990's was just a means for the business cycle to make back lost time and productivity and that the economic increase was to be short-lived. Due to the unique set of circumstances attributable to the economic boom discussed, since it was apparently anomalous, the rationale was put forth that such an economic upsurge would not recur for quite some time.

Gyurkovics, Meyer, and Takacs (2007) modeled a simulation between two players in an economy. The government and the private sector were the two players in these simulations of two-person zero-sum nonlinear difference games that were constrained by uncertainty and the players were in conflict. Given the manner in which the study was constructed, there could be no optimized solution, as in a Nash Equilibrium strategic game, but the model resulted in a number of alternate solutions and the researchers were placed in the position of having to choose the least-worst solution given by the computer model for macroeconomic policy formulation. The difference game was constructed so that the government player must engage in cost control while the private sector player was allowed to indulge in investment and private consumption. The composite macroeconomic model exhibited by player 2, or the private sector, was an aggregated group of players opposing the government during the conflict scenario in the game. Essentially, the game was fiscal policy versus private consumption in order to derive a marginal-optimal solution for the formulation of aggregate, macroeconomic, fiscal policy. The researchers determined that everything, with regard to fiscal policy formulation when the private sector and the government failed to cooperate, was essentially a goal driven trade-off with no optimal solution.

Campbell and Krane (2005) constructed a variety of models in their study to perform forecasting for the evolution of macroeconomic policy formulation. Part of the constraints in their model reflected low volatility and stable inflation from the time period of the 1980's because this implied better control issues for macroeconomic results and thus better implications for eventual fiscal policy formulation. The researchers maintained that the use of sample limits implied that they were by default restricted to a smaller number of parameters that could be used in the model's estimation of macroeconomic factors. Their literature review specified a number of economic theory objections to a larger number of parameters and thus implied that the limited parameters utilized in the model in the study were necessary. The key to this study was that the researchers were able to demonstrate that there was now a way, as a result of this study, to measure the difference between economic output and the long-run level forecasted. The implications for this are that rational agents could now adjust their consumption accordingly with prior knowledge and thus be able to impact consumption and investment in the aggregate economy changing the eventual price level in the long-run.

The Dabla-Norris and Feltenstein (2005) study was predicated upon the revelation that model simulations show that in the absence of budgetary flexibility to adjust expenditures, raising tax rates too high drives firms into the underground economy, thereby reducing the tax base. This was hardly newsworthy, but the manner in which the researchers demonstrated this assertion, through the use of model simulations, was rather interesting. The most interesting thing in this study was that the researchers used internal and external variables, both of which have the tendency to make the results of the simulations applicable to policy formulations by a government. The manner in which the variables were constructed and applied allowed the results of the simulations, through interpretation, to be used with regard to the ferreting out of tax evaders who had proceeded to partake in the underground economies of the countries in question in this study. One means at the researchers' disposal was to run the model simulations forward in time in order to predict *how much* income should be derived from *how many* taxpayers. The exemplar in this first case was a projection of eight years forward in time. The key inter-relationship was between the real GDP and the nominal exchange rate. By demonstrating that there should be no stagnation at the conclusion of seven periods, the growth was indicative of the fact that businesses have partially enjoyed proceeds from the underground economy, or have fled the tax-base completely.

Garner (2005) realized and reported in this study that the principal result of a consumption tax was that new capital was perceived to be more valuable since the tax itself seemed to minimize the value of the pre-existing capital when compared with the introduction of the new capital. With this view in mind, the researcher maintained that the proportional consumption tax reduced the actual value of pre-existing capital by almost ten percent, which in turn was deleterious to the financial position of the elderly and the wealthy since they possessed much of the pre-existing capital. However, the researcher maintained that since the tax would occur only one time, that the tax itself would be beneficial in devaluing present assets by positively improving the effects of real output. This effect was referred to as the revenue-neutral consumption tax rate and was supposed by the researcher to improve the lot of the economy in general because, since the elderly and wealthy households actually lost wealth, those households would then have to improve savings and increase work to compensate for any real losses to wealth in general.

Genberg's (2005) study focused upon adjustment lending, over a ten year period, and discussed the macroeconomic effects of that lending and how the lending promoted the growth of the economy by stimulating investment. The researcher's contention, from the results of the study and the use of simulation models, was that the growth was fostered indirectly in a non-linear manner. The old economic by-line that aid to countries to promote such economic growth was well received, when good macroeconomic policies were observed, was debunked because the aid fostered such growth indirectly and the good stewardship, intuitively assumed, that was necessarily implied was inapplicable.

Ghersi and Hourcade (2006) concluded, with regard to the prediction potential for computer modeling and simulations in particular, that the comparative-static analysis starts with ensuring that BU and TD no-policy projections portray the same world at the selected t+n horizon. In the world of energy production, projection with models has proven to be integral to the wise allocation of scarce economic resources. The previous statement assumes, or implies, that the value constructs in the simulations must be comparably applicable to the base-line for the overall energy sector at large. Without this particular model constraint, the simulation's results would be skewed. Another constraint to be observed, with relation to the adaptation of the model, was that the production and demand functions must be coordinated in order to make the results of the simulation relevant to the real world. The implication was that the entire range of energies that contain carbon that would contribute to the overall future carbon footprint that we leave as a legacy to our progeny, should be broad enough in the function equations so that they would contain all of the asymptotic behavior of energy systems. The entire basis of this entire sequence of events, with relation to the constraints placed upon the simulations performed by computer, was that the range of the carbon energies were all determined by derivatives of partial pricing determined by the demand

and production functions. The signaling of price was the primary determinant of the range specifications to make the models applicable to the real world, so the models were all price driven by partial derivatives.

Gyurkovics, Meyer, and Takacs (2007) found that, with regard to computer model simulations, a balanced budget could depend upon the model's uncertainty measure. This consideration, coupled with the modeling of the improvement of the quality of a proposed labor force, allowed the researchers to guarantee cost controls because there was no means of a guarantee in the model's simulation results without such an improvement. Further considerations were the restraints built in to the model that included an adjustable volume of capital injected into the model and the unfavorable condition of a huge amount of state debt.

Holden and Wulfsberg (2007) performed their simulations on specific data sets instead of utilizing across the board averaging of variables in the data sets. In other words, the researchers assumed no wage rigidity for the study and derived country-year data notional statistical evaluations for the data shaping the curves based upon real versus the nominal wage growth data acquired during the study. The researchers accounted and adjusted for economic advancement, shocks, and other adverse sector phenomena that affect large data sets. They then compared projected wage reductions with actual wage reductions (notional versus empirical) and they found that if the notional cuts were proportionally larger than the actual wage cuts, then the trending was toward real downward wage rigidity. Most of the previous studies had been conducted upon nominal wage rigidity, so this study was considerably different from the literature surveyed. The researchers contended that nominal downward wage rigidity had been used as an indicator in past studies because inflation served as a vehicle for a coordinated reduction in real wages (as implied by Keynes' argument for the existence of downward nominal wage rigidity). The researchers contended that the real wages were at issue (instead) and that agents in an ongoing economy should be interested in the downward real wage rigidity because of the interplay between wage rigidity and inflation. Since this affected agents' spending capital, the researchers found that this was more relevant to real world applicability and the prediction value associated with the simulation.

Kraev and Akolgo (2005) decided that there were several constraints that should be written into a model simulation to make the results effective so that the prediction would be useful for macroeconomic policy formulation:

* variable employment and capacity utilization;
* either quantity or relative price to be the dominant mode of adjustment in any given sector;
* both output and price impacts of aggregate demand; and
* an independent investment function.

Kraev and Akolgo (2005) determined, after careful study of the four major types of simulation models, econometric, computable general equilibrium, microsimulation, and fixed ratio, that the computable (CGE) model was the most desirable, but not necessarily the most accurate producer of consistent results that were useful for macroeconomic policy formulation. There were two different types of CGE model that could be used, the most current use of which has been in the government market by traders who were interested in the non-monetary market sector such as bonds. The constraints of full employment of labor and capital, sectoral adjustments driven by relative prices, and the aggregate price level being essentially driven by the money supply characterized the CGE neoclassical model whereas the constraints of quantity adjustments of output and cost-driven prices characterized the structuralist CGE model type. The researchers were unclear about which of these two types of CGE models would be optimal. They did maintain that between the two types of the general

CGE model types that most macroeconomic scenarios could be effectively modeled in developing countries. They determined that with the continued use of the CGE model, versus the other three of the four total model types examined, would sacrifice some accuracy of prediction, and that the CGE model in general would consistently generate the highest quality result for fiscal policy formulation with macroeconomic modeling of developing country economies.

This literature review essay built upon the theoretical perspectives and critical analyses presented in the Breadth component of this paper by using those macroeconomic theorists, and the applicable parts of their respective theories, as a foundation for the discussion involving the current research that was introduced in the annotations above. The integrated focus of the annotated research articles discussed above was macroeconomic theory applied to economic forecasting and computer simulations that were used by end consumers who formulated fiscal policies for aggregate economies. The outline of the organization of this literature survey included major aspects of macroeconomic theory that was applied to economic forecasting and computer simulation: size of the model; approaches to the modeling of macroeconomic policy; taxation; agent based macroeconomics; heterogeneous agents and effects on housing; space and time in a macroeconomic model; external aid on economic growth; macroeconomic consistency issues; matrix analysis of macroeconomic index fluctuations; effects of external shocks on fiscal and monetary policies; external shocks on production technologies; gaming and dimensions of macroeconomic models; forecasting with macroeconomic models; and simulations.

The rationale of the Depth narrative was to explore in detail these fourteen named aspects of economic forecasting and computer simulation, as they related to and reflected upon macroeconomics and the theories espoused in the Breadth segment, to improve the reader's understanding of these subjects and provide a foundation for analyses, comparisons, and contrasts in the Application segment of this paper.

Application

Applied Macroeconomics

Introduction

The Application component of this paper introduces a theoretical construct for use in economic forecasting and computer simulation that is as much the end product, as what was not included in the definition of such a construct. A previous paper focused principally upon the construction of software for use, but this paper will focus upon the theoretical path to the guidelines and constraints for the production of a theoretical construct that would be useful in the discussed forecasting. In this way, fiscal policies could be formulated at the governmental level to impact the aggregate economy by promoting economic growth that would improve the lifestyle of a country's citizenry.

The theories discussed in the Breadth component provided a basis for the annotations and narrative in the

Nicholas Jewczyn

Depth segment. For example, an understanding of wages and rent as variables in a model discussed in the Depth segment would have been argumentative without the theoretical foundation provided in the Breadth segment. Since the construct is as much a function of what is not included in its formulation, as what was included, a discussion in the Application of the different types of models that are in conventional use by government forecasters, economists, and econometricians is vital to the framework chosen for the theoretical model in this Application.

Although a foundation in the theoretical background associated with the economics of risk and time was not covered in the Breadth and Depth segments, it is critical to a thorough understanding in the Application segment and, for clarity, is included with some references to the subjects covered above in the Breadth and Depth components. Applied Econometrics is simply the calibration of raw data for use in economic forecasting and the various methods, conventional, accepted, and theoretical, are covered in the Application segment below. These methods interface with the theories of the Breadth and research from the Depth segments in order to promote understanding for the Application choices made for the construct. Cross section and panel data are explained as possible choices, along with the structural

150

econometrics of auction data, but are dismissed because of the value of time series data, the explanation of which is interspersed throughout the Application segment, as a better choice for this particular construct. These data types are completely explained, with references to the theories of the Breadth and research in the Depth so that the reader can realize the difference and value of the use of time series data in this proposed construct's guidelines.

A section for enhanced understanding of the critical values and a framework for understanding economic forecasts is included to demonstrate the value for the use of the construct promoted in the Application segment and this directly relates to the choice of a theoretical construct for use as a macroeconomic forecast model. This particular organization of the Application segment demonstrates the higher order understanding associated with these component parts in order to act, as an end of paper segue way, as an understanding bridge between the Breadth theories, Depth research, and the Application theoretical construct. This bridging mechanism of understanding is beyond comparison and contrast or simply an analysis of the material; it conclusively demonstrates the comprehension necessary to view theoretical plans, current research recommendations, and applied material in the field of study to put knowledge into practice so that there is a better tool available to constructively induce positive social change. This actively promotes a better governmental tool for economic forecasting so that fiscal policy is responsive, less costly, and more effective in promoting economic growth for society at large.

Economics of Risk and Time

Gollier (2001) offered a variety of guidelines for the processing of a macroeconomic model so that the results would make sense, be applicable to the real world, and be applied judiciously for the formulation of fiscal or monetary policy. Gollier described risk aversion in three different ways: "the risk itself, the wealth level of the agent and his utility function" (p. 17). There are a number of foundational issues concerning risk, but an important consideration regarding risk is the Arrow-Pratt approximation. Arrow-Pratt basically mandated that "the risk premium for a small pure risk is approximately proportional to its variance." In other words, for smaller risks, Arrow-Pratt tells us that the "risk premium is approximately proportional to the coefficient of absolute risk aversion measured at initial wealth" (p. 22). Unfortunately, as far a Macroeconomics is concerned, this proposition does not hold true for large wealth, large risk, or even large risk aversion. In fact, if the divergence of the graphs of risk premium and the risk premium approximation were observed on a graph, the two diverge at the point of (if risk is represented by *k*) *k*=4 variance such that the risk premium is also divergent. The premium diverges at *k*=4 moving above the approximation so that the larger the risk and the associated risk premium, the more underestimated the Arrow-Pratt proposition is divergent on the graph and the less coverage an agent could obtain based upon the underestimation of the risk premium for the associated risk covered (p. 23).

Gollier (2001) noted that there were a variety of rather straight-forward utility functions that described risk in different ways, but they were all reliant upon the concept of H.A.R.A., or what is described as "harmonic absolute risk aversion" (p. 26). The utility functions were: C.R.R.A., C.A.R.A., and quadratic utility functions. C.R.R.A., or "constant relative risk aversion," simply stated is the relational premium that an agent would be willing to fund if an increasing risk was not wealth dependent. C.A.R.A., or "constant absolute risk aversion," is based simply on the fact that if (*z* equals wealth) *z* approaches positive infinity, then absolute risk aversion is completely independent of wealth and the concomitant calculus function positively demonstrates an "increasing relative risk aversion." The quadratic functions are somewhat easier to use, with regard to the purview of economic agents in our fictional economy examined, but there are two principal drawbacks to the use of those quadratic functions. It was assumed in the earlier two utility functions that the premiums paid for risk aversion, the ratio of those successive premiums with relation to increasing wealth and risk, decreased. Unfortunately, with the use of quadratics, this is not so. Also, wealth is not infinite (in a positive sense, although it is possible in our present economy to have *negative* wealth), the wealth in a quadratic utility function is a positive real number "capped" at some number n. So the two drawbacks of the use of quadratic utility functions would make them inappropriate for the larger aggregates utilized in a fictional macroeconomic model for forecasting (p. 27).

Gollier (2001) suggested that there was a cost associated with forecasting with these types of utility functions in general when they were used to measure macroeconomic risks. If we were to consider a straight-forward macroeconomic model where, "every agent would be promised the same share of the aggregate production in the future. This means that the risk borne by every agent is measured by the uncertainty affecting the growth of GDP per head." This is essentially a staggering thought, since all other accumulated or divergent risks were "washed away by diversification" (p. 32). Econometrically, when the frequencies of the risks involved with this statement were transformed into the associated probabilities and the supposition was tested using decades of data, there could only be one residual conclusion associated with even the most complicated macroeconomic model used for forecasting. Since the cost of risk (socially) is expensed on a graph of GDP growth, and if we were to use an outside bound of 4% growth with regard to that U.S. GDP growth graph, then "*the macroeconomic risk does not cost us more than one-tenth of a percent of growth*" (p. 33). This essentially means that there is not enough of a cost associated with the risk internal to the model to expend even a trivial amount of time, effort or money to address the risk or diminish it.

Gollier (2001) espoused several conclusions with regard to risk in general and how that risk could be dealt with concerning macroeconomic models in particular. Gollier realized that the demand for wealth that has risk associated with it was reduced or the sub-set of risks that the agent will endure was reduced, if there was a measured rise in risks that the agent associated with these circumstances felt was intolerable. When diffidence increased when wealth was at the initial stages, then the agent decided that the level of acceptable risk needed to decrease. However, when the overall aversion to risk at the initial wealth stage was increased, then the actual demand for the wealth that had risk associated with it decreased. Overall, Gollier concluded that these two concepts were not as strong as a general rise in risk aversion and that diffidence, as a general rule, was not quite as strong as the tendency toward "central risk aversion." Gollier maintained that these concepts were developed with *hyperplane separation theorems* and that they involved mathematics and that "Jensen's inequality and the covariance rule are applications of this theorem" (pp. 95-96).

Gollier (2001) determined that an agent in an economy changes their belief and system of beliefs secondary to risk distribution and the economic "signaling" that accompanies such risk. This belief was absolutely dependent upon the fact that "expected utility is linear in the probabilities of the various states of the world" with respect to any modeled economy used for prediction. Therefore, a signal that was connected to unknown states of the economic model of the world only had value when the agent could change extant decisions predicated upon gathered information. The rationale behind this, since the malleability of the behavior was expected, was that the worst an agent, a theoretical model, or an economy could experience was the duplication "of the uninformed agent to secure the same level of expected utility" (p. 380).

Applied Econometrics

Kennedy (2003) determined that there were facets of Economics that required calibration, empirical or raw data in particular, and that this function fell to Econometrics. As opposed to what economists describe as a function, the econometrician would add certain additional measures to the relationship. Since an Economics function seldom states an exact value with accuracy, Econometrics relates the stochastic nature of the actual relationships within the function by relating by how much the answers to the function miss the "precise value" with what is referred to as the "disturbance term." The disturbance is merely the range of values that the equation could produce and expresses by how much the answer could miss the actual value sought. These disturbance errors are classified in three ways: "Omission of the influence of innumerable chance events;" "Measurement error; and "Human indeterminacy." The omission is the consequence of the economic relationship's inexactness or the fact that it was not written correctly. Measurement means that one or more of the equation's variables simply can't be accurately determined; this is secondary to data collection errors or perhaps that the variable itself simply is incapable of accurate measurement. The human factor is the randomness associated with being human and this is factored into the set or the lottery of values that the econometrician uses to describe an economic equation or set of equations. It is important to note that these three disturbances do not exist in a vacuum and that they may co-exist in the same macroeconomic simulation and could all adversely affect one another decreasing the overall accuracy of the equations chain and thus their associated, predictive value (p. 3).

Kennedy (2003) further noted, with regard to estimates and estimators in Econometrics, that there was usually more than one variable to be estimated (for accuracy) in a set of Economics equations and that there were three estimators that were conventionally used: "beta-hat;" beta-star;" and the "ordinary least squares (OLS) estimator." Set theory dictated that there was a set of values that the econometrician might use to depict the possible values for variables in a chain of Economics equations, so the range of those values was depicted by the use of these three beta estimators and the conventional one used in most texts was the beta OLS estimator. The OLS estimator represented consistency and many econometricians recognized the value set without much explanation. The focus of the equations was thus centered upon the set theory described by the estimators, since the final answers(s) to the equations chain was secondary to the quality of the estimates used to solve them. The real value of an econometrician was the inherent ability to initially choose the right estimator to resolve the answers from chain equations. Obviously, a good estimator for one equation could be a bad estimator for another equation, so the key was to choose a preferred estimator that worked for the equations in question, but not for all equations in general in order to make the solution set relevant to the situation and valuable as a predictive tool in macroeconomic computer simulations (p. 5).

Kennedy (2003) stated that the "classical linear regression model (CLR model)" is the regular model in use by econometricians and the use of that model was predicated upon five assumptions. The first was that the "dependent variable can be calculated as a linear function of a specific set of independent variables." This assumption naturally included a disturbance assessment, as previously discussed, and the ultimate answers were thus expressed as a reasonable range of answers or predictive values. The second was "that the expected value of the disturbance term is zero" (p. 47). If this were not the case, with regard to the second assumption, then there would be answer bias, a violation of the model in general, and it would necessarily relate that the mean of the disturbance term was not zero. Third, "the disturbance terms all have the same variance and are not correlated with one another." This needed to be the case. When this assumption was violated, because correlation invalidated the set theory range of answers and skewed the results, if any, the model's results were not of much worth with respect to predictive value. The fourth "is that the observations on the independent variable can be considered fixed in repeated samples." This was necessarily the case so that the equations could be repeated with the same variable data sets and the independent variable values would then be consistent. The fifth "is that the number of observations is greater than the number of independent variables and that there are no exact linear relationships between the independent variables. "Generally this is a valid assumption, but it can usually only be verified for *particular* cases under examination" (pp. 47-49).

Kennedy (2003) noted that the use of "extraneous information" could adversely affect the set theory assumptions associated with econometric analysis and the eventual predictive value of the solution set(s). Since "incorrect extraneous information creates bias, so trading off variance and bias (usually through the MSE criterion) becomes a question of central importance in this context." This type of extraneous information was supposed to improve the estimations secondary to the parameters of an equations chain, but it did not always work that way. If the introduced extraneous information reduced the variance, then such an exchange could be remarkably skewed due to the introduction of increased bias. If this became the case, econometricians used the MSE (mean square error) "criterion." Since the OLS estimator was usually utilized in the set theory of proposed ranges for the equations, "pre-test bias" occurred when, even when the appropriate specifications were used in the pre-test, the "pre-test estimators" did not result in the proper values necessary for the OLS estimator. The conventional solution to these sorts of issues was actually known by another term. Sequential hypothetical testing, or data mining, which tested large numbers of hypotheses to find a small sub-set by sorting through large numbers of independent variables by computer to find a small set of independent variables, greatly increased the possibility of choosing the wrong set of independent variables. Econometricians usually did not admit to the issues raised with the use of such methods, or they ignored them completely. For our uses of a macroeconomic model computer simulation however, the fact that these errors and biased pre-test issues occurred was important to improve the theoretical construct's credibility and perceived results. The most important consideration, with regard to these pre-test issues, was to make certain that the MSE conditions in the "pre-test estimator" were recognized and considered in order to improve the eventual value of the model's results (pp. 219-221).

Kennedy (2003) explained that the non-stationarity of variables in econometric analysis caused issues, when compared with the statisticians' time series analysis. Since "nonstationary variables have an infinite variance, inference using OLS is invalid, causing erroneous specifications to be adopted." Thus time series analysis for use in Econometrics has changed and there were several points to consider regarding time series analysis in general. Kennedy mentioned that an ARIMA model, or a "Box-Jenkins approach," was one type of time series model. When the mean changed versus time, the economic data would not be stationary. With the use of "differencing," the Box-Jenkins approach maintained that much of the economic data that could be examined could artificially be made to be "stationary" for examination. The differencing manufactured new data sets for Box-Jenkins analysis since the terms of error remained equal, with regard to percentage, they enlarged when the related variables increased. The three main steps for this ARIMA model were selection of the model, the actual estimation, and then the checking of the diagnostic relationships. The VAR is a "vector autoregression model" that combined Box-Jenkins and time series analysis. This second model type differed from the traditional Box-Jenkins model by removing the moving average constraints thus simplifying the model, but unfortunately the results as well. Some economists have described this process as "incredible," because the skewed results, although simply arrived at, were not much in line with the more traditional ARIMA model's usage. These dynamic models were somewhat successful, but there was also an "error-correction model" introduced that improved upon these other two models by the fact "that the long-run equilibrium position is not embodied in an explicit associated set of simultaneous equations but instead is represented by one or more error-correction terms." This lead to the mathematic label "error-correction model, or ECM." The ECM was a dramatic improvement over both models, but in particular over the Box-Jenkins, since the Box-Jenkins was limited by static constraints (pp.319-324).

Kennedy (2003) stated that forecasting was reliant upon good "parameter estimates" and that forecasting in general could be divided into two categories: "Causal forecasting/econometric models;" and "Time series models." The value of the causal forecasting model was that it could be used to render what most experts in the field actually considered to be an "econometric forecast." The range for this type of model was rather large in that it could employ from one equation up through a "large simultaneous-equation model with scores of variables." The time series models, conversely, were usually described by a "time trend, a seasonal factor, a cyclical element, and an error term." So the elemental series' behavior could be forecasted because each of these components could be broken out of the model to compartmentalize it, thus increasing the model's accuracy, and make the composite forecast more accurate as a result. The entire basis for a time-series model rested upon the assumption that the past was a predictor of the future and it was this assumption that was used for the collection of data for use in the model. The most common model employed in this type of forecasting was the Box-Jenkins model and when economists, differentiated from the more conventional, populist forecasters who promoted business cycle forecasting, referred to forecasts or forecasting in general, these economists generally made reference to the Box-Jenkins time-series forecasting model (p. 358). Of the seven ways of measuring forecasting accuracy, "Mean absolute deviation...root mean square error...mean absolute percentage error...correlation of forecasts with actual values...percentage of turning points forecast... quadratic score...conditional efficiency," there was no one means of determining the best model for all situations. A model was situation dependent and a forecaster must be content to choose the minimizing, of the seven error types, for the particular scenario to be addressed (pp.361-362).

Cross Section and Panel Data Analysis

Wooldridge (2002) indicated that the "single-equation linear model," after many years of considerable amounts of work in the field of Economics in general, was still consistently used in the sub-field of empirical Economics. Since the more conventional econometric response to a model was the stationary treatment of descriptive variables, the ordinary least squares approach provided a more comfortable explanatory link for a stochastic approach to the descriptive variables. When working with scalars, there was the fact extant that we attempted to estimate the unobservable error, or disturbances, and the random errors were actually the parameters that the econometrician was attempting to derive (to solve the equation or equations). A "structural model" was one that depicted a relationship that was causal, wherein the combination of advanced algebraic mathematics mixed with additional assumptions to form what was known as an "estimable model." Whichever model type was chosen for a particular set of equations, depended upon the assumptions that were originally made that were secondary to the model itself and the case scenario in question (that the econometrician was attempting to solve) (p. 49).

Wooldridge (2002) decided that there was a unique

situation that arose as a result of descriptive errors in econometric manipulation. "Endogenous explanatory variables" could complicate a model when they occurred as a result of model variables that contained "measurement error." This measurement error was reported as a consequence of the use of the ordinary least squares estimator when establishing the data ranges for the model itself. It was important to note that the eventual manifestation of the structure of the error was quite different from "variable-proxy" variables. Variable-proxy variables were contingent upon and arose from unobserved variables, but the measurement error issue was related to the fact that the unobserved variable was actually derived from a condition where the variable itself had a "well-defined, quantitative meaning." The example of such an unobserved variable could be one that arises from a sub-set that used data such as a "marginal tax rate." The measurement error actually arises from the measurement of that unobserved variable, however quantitative and well-defined it may be (p. 70).

Wooldridge (2002) realized that there were certain situations that could otherwise alter what seemed to be perfectly admissible calculations from equations that were previously useful in other scenarios. For example, in situations where voluntary participation was used in the data for the equations, such as "job training programs and school voucher programs," and the voluntary participation was assumed to be endogenous, so "participation and eligibility are correlated, the latter can be used as an IV for the former." However, this linkage suffered and became known as a "natural experiment" when the data, for some unobserved reason, became exogenous and the correlation linkage broke down. This exogenous variation, which was not originally compensated for in the error estimation skewed the eventual results because it was either unobserved, or worse, unaccounted for in the equations before modeling took place (p. 88).

Wooldridge (2002) reported that, when multiple variables were described by chain equations, that "any or all of simultaneity, omitted variables, and measurement error can be present in a system of equations." It must be added, however, that this description applied particularly to "simultaneous equations models (SEMs)." The principal factor that helped to govern applicability of these three issues centered upon the type of scenario that was appropriate for use with SEMs. Two examples offered by Wooldridge were the "labor supply and wage offer example." By the nature of the data sets involved and what the outcome was purported to be, these two were typical examples of SEMs used in the marketplace for conventional macroeconomic simulation models. It was also important to realize that when an equation could be isolated from the remaining equation chains in the model, it was said to be "autonomous," since it had stand-alone meaning and an identity of its own. The value of this characteristic of an equation was that it could be isolated from the original equations chain and, for example, be used to "trace out the individual labor supply function for given levels of the other observed and unobserved variables" (p. 209).

Wooldridge (2002) realized that, in circumstances removed from an illustrative cross sections data sample that tended to be time repetitive, a "matched pairs sample" of, for example sibling data, could be useful in research in the social sciences. This type of control was used to compensate for "unobserved family background variables" and could remarkably clean up the eventual results. If a certain hypothetical variable, let's presumptively call it the "*family effect*," was used to compensate for unobserved variables in the data set, then the factor (to prove something else) could be used to correlate arbitrarily with actual variables that were observed and formally listed in the original data sets. Then, "differencing" across the sibling set to remove that hypothetical family effect variable later, could be perceived by some to be an appropriate compensation "strategy" for the unobserved variable that surfaced during modeling (pp. 328-329).

Wooldridge (2002) promoted three "iterative schemes" that could be of use when modeling a problem where a variable was required to be minimized. The "Newton-Raphson method" was of use when the "objective function decreases" according to the nature of the starting equation's estimators and constraints. Some pitfalls in the use of this method were that the second derivative must be computed after each iterative round of calculations and if the "least squares" were non-linear, the "sum of the Hessians evaluated" might cause "the procedure" to go awry and proceed in an alternate direction (pp. 372-374). For estimates of likelihood, the "Berndt, Hall, Hall, and Hausman (BHHH)" algorithm was useful for M-estimation. It was critical to realize that this was effectual even when the "information matrix equality" issue that originally prompted the minimization problem itself was incongruent and did not "hold" (pp. 374-375). Wooldridge's third minimization iterative scheme was the "generalized Gauss-Newton method," which was very similar to the lemma wherein there was need of only the first derivatives of a mean function that was conditional. This optimization was related to regression for "nonrobust" statistics (pp 375-376).

Structural Econometrics of Auction Data

Paarsch and Hong (2006) discussed four different auction formats so that the data associated with such matrices would be more comprehensible. The "oral, ascending-price (English) format" was the particular format type with which many readers may be familiar. The process was initiated by an auctioneer who introduced a low price and then proceeded to bid up the price of an item. When the bidding finally slowed to a stop, or failed to occur at all, the auctioneer simply used a verbal mechanism, in addition to the conduct of the verbal nature of the auction itself, to close the bidding and award the item in question to one of the bidders. This type of auction has been referred to as the English auction by "economic theorists" (p. 22).

The second auction format discussed by Paarsch and Hong (2006) was the "first-price, sealed-bid format" that was the second most frequently used format. The English format was the most commonly observed format in actual, contemporary use. Unfortunately, the public in general did not seem to consider this format to be acceptable, for a variety of reasons, but economic theorists do consider this to be a valid auction type. Participants in the auction submitted a written, private bid and all of the envelopes were opened simultaneously. Whoever was the highest bidder, with regard to the price offered for an item of value, was then awarded the item in question. The reason that this type of auction format accounted for the majority of most transactions by value is that economic theorists included, under this category, procurement bids in "sealed bid tenders" in the business world. This could account for why the public did not consider this type of format to be a type of auction (p. 22).

The third type of auction discussed by Paarsch and Hong (2006) is the "oral, descending-price (Dutch) format" auction where the price of an auctioned item was set very high. As the price plummeted, bidders then activated an electronic switch and where ever the price was when the switch was activated, was what the winning bidder paid for the item under consideration. The fourth type of auction type was the "second-price, sealed-bid (Vickrey) format" auction. This auction type was similar in design to the first-price, sealed-bid, but when the bids were all opened, the winner paid the price bid by the nearest, second highest price bidder. This particular format was not very prevalent in the market, with the exception of rare stamp sales that were conducted in this auction format by mail (p. 23).

Paarsch and Hong (2006) noted that there were some disparities among the various auction types. The researchers sided with the previous findings of other researchers when they mentioned that "expected revenues under risk aversion" were different for the various auction types. Paarsch and Hong stated that the first-price and Dutch auctions have statistically proven to have higher expected revenues than Vickrey and English auctions in general. This generalization came as a result of comparison of the preponderance of risk-averse bidders with risk-neutral bidders by category that attended all four auction types in general (p. 42).

With regard to covariates, Paarsch and Hong (2006) explained that bidders in general had a fairly strong notion of what the value of a particular auctioned item might be on a personal level and what they might be willing to pay at an auction. The auctioneer, however, did not know this information and there was thus information asymmetry. If bidders were to team up and compare notes to attempt to resolve this information asymmetry, it would still hold because of the latent inefficiency of such action. This concept was referred to as the "*Myerson-Satterthwaite* theorem." The overall mentality of the auction concept was quite different from the posted price phenomenon associated with commodities that were in common usage. The real difficulty in setting auction prices, for some auction types, was that the item auctioned was a one-of-a-kind item or the items that it was compared with for pricing purposes differed by location or due to seasonality.

To attempt to compensate for these location or seasonality factors, for the comparable pricing of auction items (and by inference, auction data for econometric use), variables could be selected to control for these issues by covariate season, location or month. Then, the "quantified factors" could be controlled for by using a vector related to the "probability function" that would depend upon another particular variable. In other words, these conditionals could be used to describe and depict the covariates for use with the data to improve the accuracy of the model in question (pp. 55-56).

Paarsch and Hong (2006) discussed several factors associated with "multi-unit demand" auctions and how compensation could occur. This type of auction sub-category was dependent upon two factors regarding the demand from bidders: "*nonrandom demand* and *random demand*." In the case of nonrandom demand, without a reserve price, each of the bidders had only a weak need for the prospective, similar items offered. So, based upon a "weakly positive marginal utility," the bidders had their own idea of the auctioned items' value and ordered their purchases based upon a "cumulative distribution function." The random demand version did not assume that all of the bidders at the auction would participate, as did the nonrandom example, and the bidders were bidding on the homogeneous items randomly with no apparent goal. The valuation stream, for the bidders at this auction, was represented by a vector that weighed the marginal utility for the bidders, against the randomness of bidding with relation to the randomness of the bidding where not all of the bidders bid on all of the items. Thus, at this type of an auction, some of the items may go unsold (pp. 201-202).

Paarsch and Hong (2006) mentioned a means of resolving the auction dilemma associated with auctions in general. By conjoining vectors of valuations and "private information," there was a unique "cumulative distribution function" that described the intensity of bidding and the number of bidders and what were the assumptions of "common knowledge" that were associated with the particular auction in question. To summarize the overall bidding strategy, there was a "stopping rule" that was formal or informal based upon historical bid information and pricing in general that denoted "at what price a participant should withdraw from the current sale" (p. 209).

Understanding Economic Forecasts

Hendry and Ericsson (2003) determined that the main problem associated with forecasts in general was "systematic forecast failure that is induced by data non-stationarity" (p. 11). The editors brought forth an important point: "anything can be forecast, but not everything can be predicted" (p. 16). With regard to forecasts in general, however, the failure of a forecast was quite different from bad forecasting. There have been cases where individual and group actions in the population have changed as the result of forecasts of economic factors such as "equity prices" and the causation of "exchange-rate crises." Forecasting equations, or the models themselves, resulted from group data arising from time-series. The econometric models were usually descriptions of the inter-relationships "between variables such as GNP, inflation, money, interest rates, and exchange rates." All economic models had only three basic parts in common: "deterministic terms;" "observed stochastic variables;" and "unobserved errors." There were nine types of mistaken forecasts that could occur, based upon how these three parts were constructed and used (p. 21).

Hendry and Ericsson (2003) reported that the nine types of errors occurred in two groups: the use of "deterministic terms" and issues that involved "deterministic variables." Of the five particular errors associated with the first group type, many could be prevented through better, or even proper, preparation of the model itself. Those five errors noted for group one, with regard to deterministic terms of the model, were:

the declaration and estimates; unexpected changes; changes that described other economic changes; reducing changes effects through model construction; and revisions improving forecasts by "modeling of changes." With regard to the group two issues with forecasting models, there were four situations: "wrong slope;" intercept changes; models that persist but trends that don't; and time series and forecasts in disagreement at the "jump point." Summarizing the importance of these nine issues that could occur, with relation to forecast accuracy, improved estimation methods but did not improve accuracy (pp. 22-23).

Hendry and Ericsson (2003) demonstrated that there were two particular types of economic forecasting models, dismissing the more rudimentary models such as "rules of thumb...extrapolation; leading indicators; [and] surveys." The two main types of forecasting models were time-series and econometric models (p. 24). Due to the non-stationarity issue mentioned earlier, there were three particular formats that were generally used to construct useful models for economic forecasting: "linear trend model of output;" "constant-change model;" and the "no-acceleration model" (p. 37). The important consideration, with regard to these three model types, was that all three were remarkably different in a stochastic world and when there was a change in the rate of growth. The third model was reliable, due to the nature by which it was built, but for only the short-run (p. 38).

Hendry and Ericsson (2003) determined that there were three basic standards by which a successful forecasting model could or should be judged to determine whether or not it was a macroeconomic model that provided reliable forecasts. It was evaluated based upon "the minimum sum of squared errors for one year ahead on three forecast variables: target inflation rate...claimant-count unemployment rate...[and] the full-year growth rate of the Gross Domestic Product." The advocated reasons, for these measurements, were quite straight-forward: it was a simple way of providing a fruitful estimate and it was well related to fiscal policy formulation (p. 55).

Hendry and Ericsson (2003) noted that there were many reasons that could be addressed, but that the previous three measures were suitable means for describing what faced forecasters in general. The editors stated it in this way

> Forecasters have sometimes described their task as similar to driving in a thick fog using only the rear-view mirror, but I think that is an understatement. To make the metaphor more exact, add misted windows, an unreliable clutch, a blindfold, and handcuffs-not to mention the unsignposted cliff a hundred meters down the road. (p. 56)

The editors then described five ways to ameliorate, or cure, the difficulties in general associated with economic forecasting: "spurious precision, forecast errors, targets, uncertainty, and forecast difficulties" (p. 57).

Hendry and Ericsson (2003) decided that spurious precision was difficult to avoid completely, because people in general seemed to desire absolutes for answers to questions. This would be no different from the expectations from an economic model. So, publishers, to save space and time, will sometimes round off numbers and that then changes the accuracy of the original forecast tendered for publication. This was only one circumstance, but there were many others that could be used to illustrate the same point (p. 57). Scapegoats abound in government circles and it was not uncommon for government bureaucrats to blame an inaccurate forecast upon data errors and the like. So, forecast errors could sometimes not be avoided, since circumstances change, but since bureaucrats pay the bills for the engaged economists, the *spin* that the bureaucrat put on the results was sometimes out of the modeler's control (p. 59). Bureaucrats feel that they must somehow account to the "electorate" for the results accomplished, or that were hoping to be accomplished in an economy. However, the editors stated that basing a career upon a single indicator or economic forecast lacks good judgment and that this can be self-destructive in the long-run, since economic forecasts were not always known to be completely precise with regard to economic targets (p. 62). Eventual manifestation of a policy in an economy was subject to lag time, so basing all of an "operational policy" on the uncertainty of an economic forecast, without tempering it with some interpretation or common sense in application, could politically be a recipe for disaster (p. 63). With regard to the fifth of the five forecasting difficulties; economic forecasting was just plain difficult. The forecasting difficulties could inevitably cause rash generalizations, that eventually proved themselves to be just plain wrong. Indeed, an economic forecaster could become caught up in dealing with issues, which in an otherwise accurate forecast, would have just been proven to be simply moot (p. 65).

Hendry and Ericsson (2003) provided guidance about the choice of economic models that focused upon two major themes with regard to forecasting models in general: "A. Is a given model any good? For instance, does it represent the main features of some segment of the actual economy that is of interest? B. Which of two (or more) models is better" (p. 94)? The editors felt that the purpose of a particular model and the knowledge of how to apply it were both more important than the model chosen or the accuracy of the model in question.

Since the field of Economics inherently involves many choices, these two seem to be as relevant to the eventual disposition of a model and its accuracy as anything else suggested by the editors (p. 94).

Hendry and Ericsson (2003) showed that point forecasts involved cost minimization and that the "cost functions, the optimum point forecast f(n) is just a function of the conditional mean and conditional variance of p(n)(x)" (p. 98). However, the editors also noted that "asymmetric cost functions" were usually solved (initially) by "minimizing the integral." Although some function formulae were really not this simple to use and employ in the provision of a forecast with estimable errors, there was a cost for being inaccurate or just plain wrong. The disturbances, or what was known as "white noise properties," could contribute to this forecast error and thus make the use of the forecasting model too expensive. The residual costs, since the employed errors in the fiscal policy determinations could have a residual cost to an economy as a whole, resulted from the inherent errors translated from the forecasting model. The fiscal policies enforced upon an economy could have these additional costs, from the residuals, manifested as increased expenses associated with just being wrong (p. 98). Consider a proposed linkage between the forecast and the decisions made and enforced in an economy by policymakers. Part of the linkage issue had to do with the producer of the economic model, as compared with the consumer of the model's results, who must then formulate, based upon results interpretation, some sort of fiscal policy to deal with the economy. This may result in a *best-laid plans scenario* for disaster (p. 100).

Hendry and Ericsson (2003) pursued this line of thought with the residual costs that were associated with forecast error and how that tended to cost an economy more than might be expected. Economic forecasts on the whole were a valid means for policy formulation because they saved millions of hours of human effort. They were valuable since the computer modeled a simulation, and the model could effectively provide far more insight into scenarios that may never occur in the real world, but must inevitably be taken into account in order to eventually interpret the results and formulate sound fiscal policy. However, the model's results should not be followed blindly with the rationale that the computer "said so" as an appropriate response. The model's results needed to be interpreted and this brought back into account the thought of the results *producer* and the eventual *consumer* of the results achieved by the model in question (p. 171).

Hendry and Ericsson (2003) gave an example of the

costs of such forecast error with regard to the British government and some enforced policy decisions that were made with regard to the economy of the past. Since certain levels of economic weakness, with regard to wages and the housing cycle, remained in effect in the general economy longer than had been previously expected, the initial policy formulation, due to an error in trending, had to be reversed at some cost. It seemed that certain bureaucrats were convinced, based upon the economic model's results that were forecasted, that the disturbances in the general economy were going to be short-lived and the fiscal policy was then formulated accordingly. When the policies had to be reversed, causing administrative costs to the government and lost revenue from the economy, the costs proved to be much larger than the producers had originally estimated. It was fortuitous that these policies were able to be reversed in this illustrative case. Unfortunately, these types of costs were sometimes not reversible since the policy formulation and administration errors could persist and could adversely affect the administrative costs and economic costs for decades to come without any sign of relief (p. 179).

Choice for a Theoretical Construct
Macroeconomic Forecast Model

It was assumed in the two principal utility functions that the premiums paid for risk aversion, the ratio of those successive premiums with relation to increasing wealth and risk, decreased. Unfortunately, with the use of quadratics, this was not so. Also, wealth was not infinite (in a positive sense, although it is possible in our present economy to have *negative* wealth), the wealth in a quadratic utility function was a positive real number capped at some number *n*. So the two drawbacks of the use of quadratic utility functions would make them inappropriate for the larger aggregates utilized in a fictional macroeconomic model for forecasting. Based upon this previously addressed set of considerations, these two reasons would not support the choice of quadratic functions for large scale macroeconomic forecasting models.

Econometrically, when the frequencies of the risks involved with a macroeconomic model were transformed into the associated probabilities and the supposition was tested using decades of data, there could only be one residual conclusion associated with even the most complicated macroeconomic model used for forecasting. Since the cost of risk (socially) was expensed on a graph of GDP growth, and if we were to use an outside bound of

4% growth with regard to that U.S. GDP growth graph, then the macroeconomic risk did not cost us more than one-tenth of one percent of growth. This essentially meant that there was not enough of a cost associated with the risk internal to the model to expend even a trivial amount of time, effort or money to address the risk or diminish it. So the associated risk was minimal and we would be able to correct for that, based upon this discussion, in the theoretical construct, macroeconomic model.

Econometrics related the stochastic nature of the actual relationships within the function by relating by how much the answer to the function missed the precise value with what was referred to as the disturbance term. The disturbance was merely the range of values that the equation could produce and expressed by how much the answer could miss the actual value sought. These disturbance errors were classified in three ways: omission of the influence of innumerable chance events; measurement error; and human indeterminacy. The omission was the consequence of the economic relationship's inexactness or the fact that it was not written correctly. Measurement meant that one or more of the equation's variables simply could not be accurately determined; this was secondary to data collection errors or perhaps the variable itself simply was incapable of accurate measurement. The human factor was the randomness associated with being human and this was factored into the set or lottery of values that the econometrician used to describe an economic equation or set of equations. It was important to note that these three disturbances did not exist in a vacuum and that they may co-exist in the same macroeconomic simulation and could all adversely affect one another decreasing the overall accuracy of the equations chain and thus their predictive value. Therefore, when the theoretical construct was designed, these three considerations would need to be addressed.

The OLS estimator represented consistency and many econometricians recognized the value set without much explanation. The focus in the equations was thus centered upon the set theory described by the estimators, since the final answers(s) to the equations chain was secondary to the quality of the estimates used to solve them. The real value of an econometrician was the ability to initially choose the right estimator to resolve the answers from chain equations. Obviously, a good estimator for one equation could be a bad estimator for another equation, so the key was to choose a preferred estimator that worked for the equations in question, but not for all equations in general in order to make the solution set relevant to the situation and valuable as a predictive tool in macroeconomic computer simulations. For the construct, since the OLS estimator was a standard among economists, we would use this estimation guideline for our macroeconomic model.

The classical linear regression model (CLR model) was the regular model in use by econometricians and the use of that model was predicated upon five assumptions. The first was that the dependent variable could be calculated as a linear function of a specific set of independent variables. This assumption naturally included a disturbance assessment, as previously discussed, and the ultimate answers were thus expressed as a reasonable range of answers or predictive values. The second was that the expected value of the disturbance term was zero. If this were not the case, with regard to the second assumption, then there would be answer bias, a violation of the model in general, and it would necessarily relate that the mean of the disturbance term was not zero. Third, the disturbance terms all had the same variance and were not correlated with one another. This needed to be the case. When this assumption was violated, because correlation invalidated the set theory range of answers and skewed the results, if any, the model's results were not of much worth with respect to predictive value. The fourth was that the observations on the independent variable could be considered fixed in repeated samples. This was necessarily the case so that the equations could be repeated with the same variable data sets and the independent variable values would then be consistent. The fifth was that the number of observations was greater than the number of independent variables and that there were no exact linear relationships between the independent variables. Generally this was a valid assumption, but it could usually only be verified for particular cases under examination. Keeping these five points in mind, would improve the accuracy of the macroeconomic model for the results that would be secondary to forecasting to provide guidance for fiscal policy formulation.

The use of extraneous information could adversely affect the set theory assumptions associated with econometric analysis and the eventual predictive value of the solution set(s). Since incorrect extraneous information created bias, so trading off variance and bias (usually through the MSE criterion) became a question of central importance in this context. This type of extraneous information was supposed to improve the estimations secondary to the parameters of an equations chain, but it did not always work that way. If the introduced extraneous information reduced the variance, then such an exchange could be remarkably skewed due to the introduction of increased bias. If this became the case, econometricians used the MSE (mean square error) criterion. Since the OLS estimator was usually utilized in the set theory of proposed ranges for the equations, pre-test bias occurred when, even when the appropriate specifications were used in the pre-test, the pre-test estimators did not result in the proper values necessary for the OLS estimator. The conventional solution to these sorts of issues was actually known by another term. Sequential hypothetical testing, or data mining, which tested large numbers of hypotheses to find a small sub-set by sorting through large numbers of independent variables by computer to find a small set of independent variables, greatly increased the possibility of choosing the wrong set of independent variables.

Econometricians usually did not admit to the issues raised with the use of such methods, or they ignored them completely. For our uses of a macroeconomic model computer simulation however, the fact that these errors and biased pre-test issues occurred was important to improve the theoretical construct's credibility and perceived results. The most important consideration, with regard to these pre-test issues, was to make certain that the MSE conditions in the pre-test estimator were recognized and considered in order to improve the eventual value of the model's results. At this point, it was critical that the reader realize that the CGE model recommendation from the Depth segment above was being ignored. It should be understood that the theoretical construct econometric model, due to demonstrated specificity accuracy, since the econometric model exceeded the general but error laden use of the CGE model depicted in the current research, would be preferred for this Application segment.

Time series analysis for use in Econometrics has changed and there were several points to consider regarding time series analysis in general. An ARIMA model, or a Box-Jenkins approach, was one type of time series model. When the mean changed versus time, the economic data would not be stationary. With the use of differencing, the Box-Jenkins approach maintained that much of the economic data that could be examined could artificially be made to be stationary for examination. The differencing manufactured new data sets for Box-Jenkins analysis since the terms of error remained equal, with regard to relative percentage, they were enlarged when the related variables increased. The three main steps for this ARIMA model were: selection of the model; the actual estimation; and then checking of the diagnostic relationships. The VAR was a vector autoregression model that combined Box-Jenkins and time series analysis. This second model type differed from the traditional Box-Jenkins model by removing the moving average constraints, thus simplifying the model, but unfortunately the results as well.

Some economists have described this process as incredible because the skewed results, although simply arrived at, were not much in line with the more traditional ARIMA model's usage. These dynamic models were somewhat successful, but there was also an error-correction model introduced that improved upon these other two models by the fact that the long-run equilibrium position was not embodied in an explicit associated set of simultaneous equations but instead was represented by one or more error-correction terms. This then lead to the label of error-correction model, or ECM. The ECM was a dramatic improvement over both models, but in particular over the Box-Jenkins, since the Box-Jenkins was limited by static constraints. By demonstration, the other models were inadmissible, due to non-stationarity, but the ECM seemed to be the best choice for the construct since it dealt effectively with the OLS invalidity brought on secondary to the non-stationarity of the time-series data. Thus, by definition, the panel data and auction data examples shown herein above would not be chosen and the time-series with ECM would be the first choice for this application of a theoretical construct of a macroeconomic model for forecasting.

The main problem associated with forecasts in general was systematic forecast failure that was induced by data non-stationarity. Anything could be forecast, but not everything could be predicted. With regard to forecasts in general, however, the failure of a forecast was quite different from bad forecasting. There have been cases where individual and group actions in the population have changed as the result of forecasts of economic factors such as equity prices and the causation of exchange-rate crises. Forecasting equations or the models themselves resulted from group data arising from time-series. The econometric models were usually descriptions of the inter-relationships between variables such as GNP, inflation, money, interest rates, and exchange rates. All economic models have only three basic parts in common: deterministic terms; observed stochastic variables; and unobserved errors. There were nine types of mistaken forecast that could occur, based upon how these three parts were constructed and used. So, in the use of the ECM econometric model, we must also be cognizant of the nine types of error and deal with the biases as well as the data anomalies secondary to the use of the model for the intended forecast.

There were two particular types of economic forecasting models, dismissing the more rudimentary models such as rules of thumb, extrapolation, leading indicators, and surveys. The two main types of forecasting models were time-series and econometric models. Due to the non-stationarity issue mentioned earlier, there were three particular formats that were generally used to construct useful models for economic forecasting: linear trend model of output; constant-change model; and the no-acceleration model. The important consideration, with regard to these three model types, was that all three were remarkably different in a stochastic world and when there was a change in the rate of growth. The third model was reliable, due to the nature by which it was built, but for only the short-run. Our basic consideration of the ECM model (considerably more accurate in the long-run), which was a combination of both principal model types, that were typically discussed as time-series and econometric (since the non-stationarity issue of the stochastic data was addressed in the combination and the OLS estimator was again useful), would still be our choice for the construct.

Guidance was provided concerning the choice of economic models that focused upon two major themes with regard to forecasting models in general: A. Is a given model any good? For instance, does it represent the main features of some segment of the actual economy that is of interest? B. Which of two (or more) models is better? The purpose of a particular model and the knowledge of how to apply it were both more important than the model chosen or the accuracy of the model in question. Since the field of Economics inherently involves many choices, these two seem to be as relevant to the eventual disposition of a model and its accuracy as anything else suggested in this study.

Residual costs associated with forecast error tend to cost an economy more than might be expected. Economic forecasts on the whole were a valid means for policy formulation because they saved millions of hours of human effort. They were valuable since the computer modeled a simulation, and the model could effectively provide far more insight into scenarios that may never occur in the real world, but must be taken into account in order to eventually interpret the results and formulate sound fiscal policy. However, the model's results should not be followed blindly with the rationale that the computer *said so* as an appropriate response. The model's results need to be interpreted and this brought back into account the thought of the results *producer* and the eventual *consumer* of the results achieved by the model in question. As long as the results from the model were kept in perspective and were tempered with a common sense interpretation, then these actions should help to ameliorate the poor results from forecast error and the high social cost associated with poor fiscal policy formulation secondary to skewed model results.

Application Summary

The Application component of this paper introduced a theoretical construct for use in economic forecasting and computer simulation that was as much the end product, as what was not included in the definition of such a construct. This paper focused upon the theoretical path to the guidelines and constraints for the production of a theoretical construct that would be useful in the discussed forecasting. In this way, fiscal policies could be formulated at the governmental level to impact the aggregate economy by promoting economic growth that would improve the lifestyle of a country's citizenry.

The theories discussed in the Breadth component provided a basis for the annotations and narrative in the Depth segment. For example, an understanding of wages and rent as variables in a model discussed in the Depth segment would have been argumentative without the theoretical foundation provided in the Breadth segment. Since the construct was as much a function of what was not included in its formulation, as what was included, a discussion in the Application of the different types of models that were in conventional use by government forecasters, economists, and econometricians was vital to the framework chosen for the theoretical model in this Application.

Although a foundation in the theoretical background associated with the Economics of risk and time was not covered in the Breadth and Depth segments, it was critical to a thorough understanding in the Application segment and, for clarity, was included with some references to the subjects covered above in the Breadth and Depth components. Applied Econometrics was simply the calibration of raw data for use in economic forecasting and the various methods, conventional, accepted, and theoretical, were covered in the Application segment above. These methods interfaced with the theories of the Breadth and research from the Depth segments in order to promote understanding for the Application choices made for the construct. Cross section and panel data were explained as possible choices, along with the structural econometrics of auction data, but were dismissed because of the value of time series data, the explanation of which was interspersed throughout the Application segment, as a better choice for this particular construct. These data types were completely explained, with reference to the theories of the Breadth and research in the Depth, so that the reader could realize the difference and value of the use of time series data in this proposed construct's guidelines.

A section for enhanced understanding of the critical values and a framework for understanding economic forecasts was included to demonstrate the value for the use of the construct promoted in the Application segment and this directly related to the choice of a theoretical construct for use as a macroeconomic forecast model. This particular organization of the Application segment demonstrated the higher order understanding associated with these component parts and acted as an end of paper segue way, or more exactly, as an understanding bridge between the Breadth theories, Depth research, and the Application theoretical construct. This bridging mechanism of understanding was beyond a comparison and contrast or simply an analysis of the material; it conclusively demonstrated the comprehension necessary to view theoretical plans, current research recommendations, and applied material in the Economics field of study to put knowledge into practice so that there was a better tool available to constructively induce positive social change. This actively promotes a better governmental tool for economic forecasting so that fiscal policy is responsive, less costly, and more effective in promoting economic growth for society at large. Although this may prove to be a platform for further research, it is postulated that further research is necessary in this field to promote the development of an actual tool for practical application in society as a whole.

References

Brown, J. (1999). *Quick course in Microsoft Excel.* Redmond, WA: Microsoft Press.

Campbell, J., & Krane, S. (2005). Consumption based macroeconomic forecasting. *Economic Perspectives, 29*(4), 52-70. Accession Number: 19121456, 2008, from Business Source Premier database.

Chen, S. (2005). Trends in agent-based computational modeling of macroeconomics. *New Generation Computing, 23*(1), 3-11. Accession Number 15621275, 2008, from Academic Search Premier database.

Dabla-Norris, E., & Feltenstein, A. (2005). The underground economy and its macroeconomic consequences. *The Journal of Policy Reform, 8*(2), 153-174. DOI: 10.1080/13841280500086388, 2008, from Academic Search Premier database.

Foote, C. (2007). Space and time in macroeconomic panel data: Young workers and unemployment revisited. *Research Review, 8*, 16-18. Accession Number 31589110, 2008, from Academic Search Premier database. Working paper of the Federal Reserve Bank of Boston, W-07-10. Full text downloaded from http://www.bos.frb.org/economic/wp/wp2007/wp0710.pdf.

Friedman, M., & Schwartz, A. (1963, 1993). *A monetary history of the United States, 1867-1960.* Princeton: Princeton University Press.

Friedman, M. (1962, 2002). *Capitalism and freedom.* Chicago: The University of Chicago Press.

Friedman, M. (1953). *Essays in positive economics.* Chicago: The University of Chicago Press.

Garner, C. (2005). Consumption taxes: Macroeconomic effects and policy issues. *Economic Review, 90*(2), 5-29. Accession Number 17386035, 2008, from Business Source Premier database.

Genberg, H. (2005). The macroeconomic effects of adjustment lending: A review and evaluation. *The Journal of Policy Reform, 8*(1), 1-40. DOI: 10.1080/1384128042000328923, 2008,from Business Source Premier database.

Ghersi, F., & Hourcade, J. (2006). Macroeconomic consistency issues in e3 modeling: The continued fable of the elephant and the rabbit. *The Energy Journal; Hybrid Modeling of Energy-Environme, 27,* 39-61. Accession Number 23914016, 2008, from Business Source Premier.

Gligor, M., & Ausloos, M. (2007). Cluster structure of eu-15 countries derived from the correlation matrix analysis of macroeconomic index fluctuations. *The European Physical Journal, 57*(2), 139-146. DOI: 10.1140/epjb/e2007-00132-5, 2008, from Academic Search Premier.

Gollier, C. (2001) *The economics of risk and time.* Cambridge, MA: The MIT Press.

Gottschalk, R. (2005). The macro content of prsps: Assessing the need for a more flexible macroeconomic policy framework. *Development Policy Review, 23*(4), 419-442. DOI: 10.1111/j.1467-7679.2005.00295.x, 2008, from Academic Search Premier database.

Gyurkovics, E., Meyer, D., & Takacs, T. (2007). Budget balancing in a two-dimensional macroeconomic model. *Mathematical and Computer Modelling of Dynamical Systems, 13*(2), 179-192. DOI: 10.1080/13873950600739034, 2008, from Academic Search Premier database.

Hendry, D., & Ericsson, N. (Ed.). (2003). *Understanding economic forecasts.* Cambridge, MA: The MIT Press.

Hicks, J. (1969). *A theory of economic history.* Oxford: Oxford University Press.

Hicks, J. (1939, 1991). *Value and capital.* Oxford: Clarendon Press.

Holden, S., & Wulfsberg, F. (2007). How strong is the macroeconomic case for downward real wage rigidity? *Research Review, 7*, 22-24. Accession Number 26614456, 2008, from Academic Search Premier database. Working paper of the Federal Reserve Bank of Boston, W-07-6. Full text downloaded from http://www.bos.frb.org/economic/wp/wp2007/wp0706.pdf.

Ireland, P., & Schuh, S. (2006). Productivity and U.S. macroeconomic performance: Interpreting the past and predicting the future with a two-sector real business cycle model. *Research Review, 5*, 22-24. Accession Number 23674768, 2008, from Academic Search Premier database. Working paper of the Federal Reserve Bank of Boston, No. W-06-10. Full text downloaded from http://www.bos.frb.org/economic/wp/wp2006/wp0610.pdf

Jeske, K. (2005). Macroeconomic models with heterogeneous agents and housing. *Economic Review, 90*(4), 39-56. Accession Number 19489004, 2008, from Academic Search Premier database.

Kennedy, P. (2003). *A guide to econometrics.* Cambridge, MA: The MIT Press.

Keynes, J. (1924, 2000). *A tract on monetary reform.* New York: Prometheus Books.

Keynes, J. (1930). *A treatise on money.* New York: Harcourt, Brace and Company.

Keynes, J. (1920, 2006). *A treatise on probability*. New York: Prometheus Books.

Keynes, J. (1926, 2004). *The end of laissez-faire: The economic consequences of the peace*. New York: Prometheus Books.

Keynes, J. (1936, 1997). *The general theory of employment, interest, and money*. New York: Prometheus Books.

Kraev, E., & Akolgo, B. (2005). Assessing modelling approaches to the distributional effects of macroeconomic policy. *Development Policy Review, 23*(3), 299-312. DOI: 10.1111/j.1467-7679.2005.00288.x, 2008, from Academic Search Premier database.

Makasheva, N. (2006). Once again about the revolution of J.M. Keynes (An attempt to construct a macroeconomic theory for an uncertain economy, *Social Sciences, 37*(4), 16-29. Accession Number 23293723, 2008, from Academic Search Premier database.

Marshall, A. (1923, 2003). *Money, credit and commerce*. New York: Prometheus Books.

Marshall, A. (1920, 1997). *Principles of economics*. New York: Prometheus Books.

Mayes, T., & Shank, T. (2004). *Financial analysis*. Mason, OH: Thomson, South-Western.

Paarsch, H., & Hong, H. (2006). An introduction to the structural econometrics of auction data. Cambridge, MA: The MIT Press.

Ragsdale, C. (2008). *Spreadsheet modeling & decision analysis* (5th ed.). Canada: Louiseville Gagne Canada.

Ricardo, D. (1817). *The principles of political economy and taxation*. New York: Dover.

Samuelson, P. (1948, 1995). *Economics*. New York: McGraw-Hill, Inc.

Schumpeter, J. (1942, 2008). *Capitalism, socialism, and democracy*. New York: Oxford University Press.

Schumpeter, J. (1934, 1961). *The theory of economic development*. New York: Oxford University Press.

Smith, A. (1776, 2003). *An inquiry into the nature and causes of the wealth of nations*. New York: Bantam Books.

Spiegel, M. (1999). *Mathematical handbook of formulas and tables*. New York: McGraw-Hill.

Spiegel, M., Schiller, J., & Srinivasan, R. (2000). *Probability and statistics* (2nd ed.). New York: McGraw-Hill.

Wooldridge, J. (2002). *Econometric analysis of cross section and panel data*. Cambridge, MA: The MIT Press.